# GETTING INTO FILM AND TV

## JOHN BURDER

**SALTCOATS PUBLISHING**

7 SALTCOATS ROAD
LONDON W4 1AR
TEL 0181 747 0864
FAX 0181 995 3376

First published by Saltcoats Publishing , 1994

*ALSO AVAILABLE BY THE SAME AUTHOR*

**THE TECHNIQUE OF EDITING 16MM FILMS - 5TH EDITION**
**(Focal Press)**

**16MM FILM CUTTING (Focal Press)**

**WORK OF THE INDUSTRIAL FILM MAKER ( Focal Press)**

*COPYRIGHT 1994 JOHN BURDER*

All rights reserved. No part of this publication may be reproduced or transmitted in any form or by any means, including photocopying and recording without the written permission of the copyright holder. applications for which should be addressed to the Publishers. Such written permission must also be obtained before any part of this publication is stored in a retrieval system of any nature.
This book is sold subject to the Standard Conditions of Sale of Net Books and may not be re-sold in the UK below the net price given by the Publishers in their current price list.

---

BRITISH LIBRARY CATALOGUING IN PUBLICATION DATA
Burder, John
GETTING INTO FILM AND TV
ISBN 0 9523890 0 2

---

Cover design David Lewis Hall
Printed and bound in Great Britain by Chartered Press

# GETTING INTO FILM AND TV

## PREFACE

If the letters I and other television producers receive are anything to go by, there are a lot of people who want to work in film and television. If you are one of those people this book should help you. It will not make you a Producer overnight but it should help you to acquire skills which could put you ahead in the very competitive business of getting your first job.

If you do not have any experience of making films or videos you are unlikely to stand much of a chance of getting an interview let alone a job. On the other hand, if you can produce tangible evidence that you have taken the trouble to learn as much as possible and, as a result, know what you are talking about, you are likely to get a more positive response. In this book I have tried to explain what is involved in making videos and films to professional quality standards. I have assumed you know little or nothing about film or video when you start chapter one. By the end of the book I hope you will have acquired enough basic knowledge to make a showreel which will help you to get a job. It contains all the information I would have liked to have had when I started my career. If you want to perform in front of the cameras this book is not for you. If you want to be a Director or one of the other key technicians involved making films or tv programmes I hope you will find it helpful.

JOHN BURDER

# CONTENTS

**Preface.**

## CHAPTER 1 - THE OPPORTUNITIES AVAILABLE

| | |
|---|---|
| THE FIRST INTERVIEW | 1 |
| WHAT FUTURE FOR YOU ? | 3 |
| TARGETING THE RIGHT JOB | 3 |
| DEFINING YOUR AMBITIONS | 4 |
| WORKING WITHOUT GLAMOUR | 6 |
| AN ESSENTIAL QUALIFICATION | 7 |
| CONFIRMING YOU AMBITIONS | 7 |
| HOW TO BE A DIRECTOR | 8 |
| OTHER KEY JOBS | 9 |
| WORKING AS A CAMERAMAN | 9 |
| LIFE AS A SOUND RECORDIST | 10 |
| A DEAD END JOB ? | 11 |
| THE IMPORTANCE OF EDITING | 12 |
| VIDEO EDITING | 12 |
| A DIVERSE INDUSTRY | 13 |
| FEATURE FILMING | 14 |
| MAKING DOCUMENTARIES & TV PROGRAMMES | 14 |
| PRODUCING CINEMA AND TV COMMERCIALS | 15 |
| TV NETWORKS & INDEPENDENT COMPANIES | 15 |
| WORKING FREELANCE | 16 |
| BACK TO SCHOOL ? | 16 |
| WASTING THREE YEARS ? | 17 |
| CHECKING SCHOOLS TRACK RECORDS | 18 |
| WORK EXPERIENCE | 18 |
| JOINING A UNION | 19 |
| GETTING THE RIGHT QUALIFICATIONS | 20 |
| SELLING YOUR TALENTS | 20 |
| PROOF OF INTERESTS AND AMBITIONS | 20 |

## CHAPTER TWO - PLANNING YOUR SHOWREEL

| | |
|---|---|
| WHO PAYS ? | 23 |
| BORROWING FROM A BANK | 23 |
| CHOOSING THE RIGHT SUBJECT | 24 |
| BEING TOO AMBITIOUS | 25 |
| A TALENT SPOTTING EXERCISE | 26 |

| | |
|---|---|
| MAKING A DULL SUBJECT INTERESTING | 27 |
| FINDING A SPONSOR | 28 |
| SELLING IDEAS TO SPONSORS | 29 |
| FILM OR VIDEO ? | 30 |
| WORKING ON FILM | 30 |
| VIDEO STANDARDS | 31 |
| CHOOSING THE RIGHT FORMAT | 33 |
| PUTTING QUALITY FIRST | 34 |
| ONE INCH TAPE AND BETACAM SP | 35 |
| PAYING FOR QUALITY | 35 |
| GOOD QUALITY ON A TIGHT BUDGET | 36 |
| OTHER VIDEO FORMATS | 36 |
| MIXING FORMATS | 37 |
| WORKING ON U-MATIC | 37 |
| SUMMARY | 39 |
| PRODUCING A BUDGET | 39 |
| SCRIPT | 39 |
| ARTISTES | 40 |
| PRODUCER / DIRECTOR FEES | 41 |
| SALARIES (TECHNICIANS) | 42 |
| SETS AND LOCATIONS | 42 |
| LIGHTING | 42 |
| CAMERA EQUIPMENT HIRE | 42 |
| SOUND EQUIPMENT HIRE | 44 |
| WARDROBE | 44 |
| MUSIC | 45 |
| FILM/TAPE STOCK AND PROCESSING | 46 |
| EDITING | 49 |
| TRAVEL AND TRANSPORT | 51 |
| INSURANCE | 51 |
| PROFIT AND OVERHEAD | 53 |

## <u>CHAPTER 3 - DEVELOPING YOUR IDEAS</u>

| | |
|---|---|
| ATTEMPTING THE IMPOSSIBLE | 55 |
| CHOOSING THE RIGHT TREATMENT | 57 |
| TREATMENTS AND SCRIPTS | 57 |
| A SPONSOR'S BRIEF | 58 |
| WHOSE POINT OF VIEW ? | 58 |
| AN ALTERNATIVE OPENING | 59 |
| WINNING AUDIENCE INTEREST | 60 |
| PLANNING YOUR SOUNDTRACK | 61 |

| | |
|---|---|
| SYNCHRONISED AND WILD DIALOGUE | 62 |
| WORKING WITHOUT A COMMENTARY | 63 |
| BRINGING ARGUMENTS TO LIFE | 64 |
| TELLING A STORY IN PICTURES AND SOUNDS | 65 |
| PLANNING INTERVIEWS | 66 |
| MAINTAINING A COMMERCIAL SENS | 66 |
| TESTING YOUR CREATIVITY | 66 |
| MAKING A SCHOOL VIDEO | 68 |
| ORIGINAL TREATMENTS FOR WELL EXPLORED SUBJECTS | 68 |
| A DIFFERENT APPROACH | 69 |
| USING A PERSONAL VIEW FOR NARRATION | 69 |
| ALTERNATIVE WAYS | 70 |
| FROM TREATMENT TO SCRIPT | 71 |
| CHOOSING THE RIGHT VIEWPOINT | 71 |
| LOCATION "RECCYS" | 76 |
| FILMING IN PUBLIC PLACES | 77 |
| A SOUND "RECCY" | 77 |
| ANYTHING TO PAY ? | 78 |
| PREPARING A SHOOTING SCHEDULE | 78 |
| TOO MUCH PAPERWORK ? | 79 |
| A REALISTIC SCHEDULE | 80 |
| INTERNATIONAL SHOOTING | 80 |
| SUMMARY | 81 |
| SHOOTING A TEST | 82 |

## CHAPTER 4 - IN PRODUCTION

| | |
|---|---|
| ESTABLISHING A BASE | 83 |
| CHOOSING THE RIGHT LIGHTS | 84 |
| USING LIGHTS CREATIVELY | 84 |
| LIGHTING ACCESSORIES | 85 |
| INDIRECT LIGHTING | 86 |
| ASSESSING COLOUR TEMPERATURES | 86 |
| PROBLEMS WITH MIXED LIGHT | 87 |
| BALANCING DAYLIGHT | 87 |
| CAMERA FILTERS | 88 |
| USING A WHITE BALANCE | 88 |
| CORRECTING COLOURS AFTER SHOOTING | 89 |
| GOLDEN RULES FOR GOOD COLOUR BALANCE | 89 |
| WORKING WITHOUT DAYLIGHT | 90 |
| LIGHTING CHECKS | 90 |
| SHOOTING IN LOW LIGHT LEVELS | 92 |

| | |
|---|---|
| BOOSTING A VIDEO SIGNAL | 92 |
| USING HIGH SPEED FILM STOCK | 93 |
| FORCING FILM | 94 |
| PROCESSING FORCED ROLLS | 94 |
| FOCUS | 95 |
| DEPTH OF FIELD | 95 |
| FOCUS AND LENSES OF DIFFERENT FOCAL LENGTH | 97 |
| BACK FOCUS | 97 |
| CHECKING A VIDEO CAMERA | 97 |
| ADJUSTING A VIEW-FINDER | 98 |
| CHECKING BACK FOCUS | 98 |
| PROTECTING THE LEN | 99 |
| MOBILITY WITH VIDEO CAMERAS | 100 |
| VIDEO CAMERA CONTROLS | 100 |
| BUILT IN FILTERS | 101 |
| FILM CAMERA CHARACTERISTICS | 102 |
| USING A CHANGING BAG | 103 |
| FILM RUNNING SPEEDS | 104 |
| ASSESSING THE CORRECT EXPOSURE | 104 |
| AVOIDING PROBLEMS WITH COUPLED EXPOSURE METERS | 106 |
| CAMERA MOVEMENTS | 107 |
| ZOOMS AND TRACKS | 109 |
| LAST MINUTE CHECKS | 109 |
| IDENTIFYING EACH TAKE | 111 |
| SYNC SOUND SHOOTING | 112 |
| SYNCHRONISING SOUND AND PICTURE | 112 |
| END BOARDS & SUBSTITUTES | 113 |
| SOUND ON FILM | 114 |
| EXPECT THE UNEXPECTED | 114 |
| CROSSING THE LINE | 116 |
| CUTAWAYS | 117 |
| SHOOTING INTERVIEWS | 118 |
| SHOOTING REVERSES | 120 |
| TELE PROMPTERS | 121 |
| SHOOTING SPECIAL EFFECTS | 122 |
| SLOW MOTION | 122 |
| USING A VARIABLE SPEED SHUTTER | 123 |

## **CHAPTER 5 - POST PRODUCTION**

| | |
|---|---|
| EDITING AND COMMERCIAL SUCCESS | 125 |
| EDITING - AN AMATEUR VIEW | 125 |

| | |
|---|---|
| A CRUCIAL STAGE | 126 |
| THE RESULT OF BAD EDITING | 126 |
| UNCUT RUNNING TIME | 128 |
| SEX IN EDITING | 129 |
| LOGGING RUSHES | 129 |
| VIDEO POST PRODUCTION - THE MAIN STAGES | 130 |
| FILM POST PRODUCTION - THE MAIN STAGES | 131 |
| WHY COPY UNCUT MASTER TAPES ? | 131 |
| FILM AND VIDEO EDITING COMPARED | 133 |
| ON LINE EDITING - THE BASIC PRINCIPLE | 133 |
| ANCILLARY ON LINE EQUIPMENT | 134 |
| THE COST OF WORKING ON LINE | 135 |
| OFF LINE - THE BASIC PRINCIPLES | 135 |
| CUTTING ON FILM - THE BASIC PRINCIPLES | 137 |
| WHY NOT CUT THE MASTER ? | 137 |
| CUTTING WITHOUT A SCRIPT | 140 |
| ENCOURAGING AUDIENCES TO WATCH & LISTEN | 141 |
| PLANNING A SEQUENCE | 142 |
| PREPARING YOUR EDIT MASTER | 145 |
| IDENTIFYING YOUR MASTER TAPE | 146 |
| YOUR OPENING SHOT | 147 |
| USING AN EDIT CONTROLLER | 148 |
| CHOOSING THE RIGHT EDIT MODE | 149 |
| SELECTING EFFECTS TYPE | 150 |
| IDENTIFYING THE CORRECT IN POINT | 150 |
| SELECTING THE IN POINT ON YOUR RECORDER | 151 |
| MAKING THE SAME EDIT OFF LINE | 152 |
| CONTINUITY IN CUTTING | 152 |
| EDIT DECISION LISTS | 153 |
| THE PROCEDURE OFF LINE | 153 |
| AVOIDING DOUBLE TAKES | 154 |
| CUT OR DISSOLVE ? | 155 |
| CUTTING CAMERA MOVEMENTS | 155 |
| OVERLAPS FOR DISSOLVES | 156 |
| OFF LINE DISSOLVES | 157 |
| DISSOLVES FOR SCENES SHOT ON THE SAME ROLL | 157 |
| WHEN TO CUT ? | 158 |
| OVERLAYING VIDEO SOUND | 159 |
| SOUNDTRACKS ON AND OFF LINE | 160 |
| THE IMPORTANCE OF BACKGROUND SOUNDS | 160 |
| REPLACING UNSUITABLE SOUNDS | 161 |

| | |
|---|---|
| SOUND AND PICTURE CUTTING POINTS | 162 |
| OVERLAYING AN INTERVIEW | 162 |
| MAKING LONG INTERVIEWS CONCISE | 163 |
| NATURAL BREAKS | 165 |
| ELIMINATING UNWANTED WORDS | 166 |
| USING THE SAME TECHNIQUES FOR OTHER SUBJECTS | 166 |
| EDITING ETHICS | 167 |
| WHERE TO CUT ? | 168 |
| ELIMINATING JUMP CUTS | 169 |
| ADDING TITLES | 170 |
| CAPTION GENERATORS | 170 |
| CREATING A SUB TITLE | 171 |
| FADING CAPTIONS IN AND OUT | 172 |
| KEYING IN | 172 |
| EFFECTS TYPES | 173 |
| EFFECTS WHEN EDITING OFF LINE | 174 |
| PUTTING ADVICE INTO PRACTICE | 175 |

## CHAPTER 6 - CUTTING ON FILM

| | |
|---|---|
| WORKING WITHOUT A VIDEO ASSIST | 176 |
| PROCESSING YOUR ORIGINAL | 177 |
| PRINTING RUSHES (DAILIES) | 178 |
| FILM POST PRODUCTION - WHAT IT INVOLVES | 179 |
| EDITING TIME | 179 |
| EDITING MACHINES - UPRIGHT MODELS | 179 |
| TABLE EDITING MACHINES | 180 |
| SYNCHRONISERS | 181 |
| JOINING FILM | 181 |
| CUTTING ROOM CONSUMABLES | 182 |
| SYNCHRONISING RUSHES | 182 |
| USING BUILD UP | 184 |
| EDGE NUMBERS | 184 |
| LOGGING FILM RUSHES | 185 |
| SELECTING THE RIGHT SCENES AND TAKES | 186 |
| BREAKING DOWN RUSHES | 186 |
| MAKING A FIRST ASSEMBLY | 187 |
| WHERE TO CUT ? | 187 |
| HOW LONG FOR EACH SHOT ? | 188 |
| CUTTING A SEQUENCE | 189 |
| USING LEADERS | 190 |
| FILM FOOTAGES | 191 |

| | |
|---|---|
| STARTING TO CUT | 191 |
| OVERLAYING DIALOGUE ON FILM | 192 |
| OPTICAL EFFECTS ON FILM | 192 |
| A & B ROLLS | 193 |
| ORDERING SINGLE ROLL OPTICALS | 193 |
| SUPERIMPOSED TITLES ON FILM | 194 |

## CHAPTER 7 - THE FINISHING TOUCHES

| | |
|---|---|
| MAKING A FINE CUT | 196 |
| LAYING SOUNDTRACKS ON FILM | 198 |
| SOUND DUBBING | 199 |
| TRACK LAYING ON VIDEO | 200 |
| EDITING SOUND OFF LINE | 200 |
| CREATING VIDEO SOUNDTRACKS ON FILM | 202 |
| VOICE OVER NARRATION (COMMENTARY) | 203 |
| GOOD AND BAD COMMENTARY WRITING | 203 |
| WHEN AND HOW TO RECORD A COMMENTARY | 205 |
| RECORDING WILD AND TO PICTURE | 205 |
| MANAGING A RECORDING SESSION | 207 |
| CONTRACTING THE RIGHT ARTISTES | 207 |
| ADDING MUSIC | 208 |
| CUTTING TO MUSIC | 208 |
| FOREIGN LANGUAGE VERSIONS | 209 |
| M & E TRACKS | 210 |
| DUBBING COMMENTARIES IN OTHER LANGUAGES | 210 |
| DUBBING OVER INTERVIEWS | 211 |
| MAKING COPIES OF YOUR FINAL EDITED VERSION | 212 |
| PRODUCING VIDEO COPIES | 212 |
| VIDEO COPIES IN DIFFERENT FORMATS | 213 |
| FILM COPIES OF VIDEOS | 214 |
| SOUND FOR FILM COPIES OF VIDEOS | 215 |
| FILM AND VIDEO COPIES OF PRODUCTION SHOT ON FILM | 215 |
| MAGNETIC AND OPTICAL SOUNDS | 216 |
| SOUND ADVANCE FOR COMOPT FILM COPIES | 217 |

## CHAPTER 8 - SELLING YOURSELF

| | |
|---|---|
| ASSESSING YOUR OWN WORK | 219 |
| A PROFESSIONAL APPRAISAL | 220 |
| APPLYING FOR A JOB | 220 |
| FOLLOWING UP YOUR APPLICATION | 224 |

| | |
|---|---|
| WORKING WITH OTHERS | 225 |
| JOB INTERVIEWS | 225 |
| ASSESSING THE SUCCESS OF YOUR SHOWREEL | 227 |
| TAKING A COMMERCIAL VIEW | 228 |
| YOUR OWN BUSINESS ? | 229 |
| STARTING A BUSINESS | 229 |
| CHOOSING A PARTNER | 230 |
| RENTING BUSINESS PREMISES | 232 |
| CHECKING A LEASE | 233 |
| ACQUIRING EQUIPMENT | 233 |
| BUY, HIRE OR LEASE ? | 234 |
| EQUIPPING YOUR OFFICE | 235 |
| BUYING A COMPUTER | 235 |
| MANAGING YOUR ACCOUNTS | 236 |
| ISSUING INVOICES | 237 |
| COSTING YOUR WORK | 238 |
| WORKING OUT YOUR HOURLY RATE | 238 |
| OTHER COSTS TO CONSIDER | 239 |
| MAKING THE BEST USE OF YOUR TELEPHONE | 241 |
| CHOOSING THE WORK YOU WANT TO DO | 241 |
| MAKING MONEY FREELANCE | 242 |
| OFFERING A PRODUCTION SERVICE | 242 |
| MAKING PRODUCTIONS FOR TV COMPANIES | 243 |
| WHAT TV COMPANIES WANT | 243 |
| SELLING IDEAS TO TELEVISION | 244 |
| MAKING FILMS & VIDEOS FOR GENERAL SALE | 246 |
| CHOOSING THE RIGHT SUBJECTS | 246 |
| BUDGETING FOR PROMOTION | 247 |
| ADVERTISING IN THE PRESS | 247 |
| SELLING BY DIRECT MAIL | 248 |
| FREE PUBLICITY | 249 |
| FILM AND TV FESTIVALS | 249 |
| PREVIEWING YOUR PRODUCTIONS | 250 |
| ARRANGING A PRESS SHOW | 251 |
| STAGING YOUR OWN PREVIEW | 252 |
| SELLING YOUR SERVICES TO SPONSORS | 253 |
| WORKING WITH SPONSORS | 253 |
| WHO KEEPS CONTROL ? | 254 |
| ARRANGING PROGRESS PAYMENTS | 255 |

**DIRECTORY OF FILM SCHOOLS, PRINCIPAL TV COMPANIES AND OTHER SOURCES OF INFORMATION**

# CHAPTER 1
# THE OPPORTUNITIES AVAILABLE

So you want to work in film or television. Welcome aboard! In the following pages I am going to try to help you satisfy your ambitions. It will not be easy. As you have probably already discovered, a lot of people want to follow the same course. They all envisage making pots of money. Some succeed. Others are doomed to fail because they do not have the necessary skills and knowledge. If you have decided that a career in banking or insurance may not provide the excitement you need and want to do something which is creative, this book is designed to help you on your way. The information it contains is all based on first hand experience. For me, as it probably will for you, acquiring that experience started with a preliminary interview.

## THE FIRST INTERVIEW

I had been warned it would be tough. "Note the way the door handle turns. It's a catch question to see if you're on the ball", one friend had advised me. "Wear a suit and a plain coloured tie so you don't upset anyone", someone else had volunteered. And there I was. After months of writing applying for jobs I had at last been invited to a preliminary interview. I reported to the BBC Television Appointments Board hoping that the ambitions I had held for so long were at last going to be given the encouragement I felt they deserved. Six sober suited men faced me as I entered the room and from the Chairman's first remark my confidence was shattered.

" You have applied for a post as a Trainee Assistant Editor. How many other applications do you think we have had to consider"? It was one question I had not expected to be asked and I had no idea how to answer. I knew I had to give some sort of reply so I picked a figure at random.

"A hundred and fifty", I suggested.

"Not quite, the Chairman replied. " As you know it took us some time to respond to your application. That was because we had two thousand three hundred and five others to consider". I was appalled. What chance had I with no professional experience and very little technical knowledge. How did I ever manage to get as far as this interview ? I could not imagine. The Chairman was a benevolent man. Seeing my face turning purple he tried to build up my confidence.

" Don't let that worry you. I should also explain that there are six vacancies on our training scheme so it not quite as bad as you might first imagine". At least he had a sense of humour. I was by now quite convinced that the following day I would again be writing letters when I heard the Chairman say.

" You are here because we were impressed by the showreel you sent us. Perhaps you could tell us how you made it". At last I had question I could answer. At school I had been far more interested in taking photographs and making a school film than I had been in any academic subjects. When I left, I had done all I could to build on that interest. I had read books, contacted professional film makers and tried to persuade them to see me and allow me to watch them at work. I had also produced a ten minute film using borrowed equipment and taking full advantage of a lot of other peoples' goodwill. I had learned a great deal making that production. It wasn't a masterpiece but it had been made for about the same cost as four meals for two at a good restaurant. I had sent it along with my application form and that, it transpired, had been a good move.

## WHAT FUTURE FOR YOU ?

Three weeks after that interview I received a letter telling me I had got the job and that was the start of a career I would not have missed for anything. If you want to follow a similar course you may well find yourself facing an interview like the one I have just described. If you do, you must be prepared. You will need to know enough about the sort of work you are applying to do to convince others that you are worth employing. If you can produce evidence of that knowledge in the form of a showreel you will find you are more likely to succeed. In the following pages I am going to try to help you acquire that knowledge and learn the skills you need to make a showreel. Then you will be able to take the first steps up the ladder which will enable you to build a career for yourself in film or television.

## TARGETING THE RIGHT JOB

You can earn your living in film and tv in many different ways. You can appear in front of the cameras as an actor or actress, newsreader, interviewer or a performer of some other kind. Alternatively you can work behind the scenes as a director, cameraman, sound recordist or editor or exercising some of the many other skills needed to produce a professional production. If those possibilities do not appeal to you you could get a job providing catering services, working as an accountant or hiring equipment or facilities. In one book it is obviously impossible to do justice to such a wide range of different interests so I have assumed that you are going to want to be programme maker. You want to make money but you also want to be "in production". I therefore intend to concentrate on subjects which will help you if you want to become part of a professional production team. That may eventually mean being a director, a cameraman or an editor, or simply doing a good job as an assistant in a production department. If that is where your ambitions lie you will find it is in your interests to read on but before we go any further, there is one question you should ask yourself. Are you sure that getting into film or television is what you *really* want to do? Are you absolutely certain that it is your real ambition, or are you just interested in what you may misguidedly think is a glamorous career ?

## DEFINING YOUR AMBITIONS

You may find it is easier to arrive at an objective answer if you consider another question at the same time. How do you see yourself in the industry you want to enter? Do you envisage a director sitting in a chair with your name on the back of it shouting "cut", while troupes of beautiful actresses await your next command ? If that is how you see yourself, you may as well put this book back on the shelf and forget it because you are almost certain to be disappointed. I can give you a much more realistic idea of what the work may be like from my experiences last week.

We were shooting a thirty second commercial on an old railway line in the depths of the country. It had rained all day and we were marooned on an open stretch of track a long way from the most basic home comforts. The script was based on an old silent classic suitably updated to include a mention of the sponsor's product. A heroine was tied to the railway line while an old steam train raced towards her. At the same time a veteran car chugged along a road running parallel to the track. At the appropriate moment the driver of the car saw the lady tied to the line, leapt from his car and raced across to untie her before the train could reach her. In the final shot the train screeched to a halt a few metres from where the heroine was lying. All good clean fun and, on paper at least, quite straightforward. After weeks of planning I and the rest of the crew had arrived at the location just after dawn. The artistes had changed into period costumes and after the usual hectic last minute preparations, shooting had begun.

For most of the morning work proceeded as planned but after lunch everything started to go wrong. One good take was ruined when drops of rain blew on to the lens. A modern jet plane appeared in the background. The old car refused to start on numerous occasions and when we at last seemed to have a take in which everything was right, the cameraman found a large hair in the camera gate so we had to go back to the start all over again. We were soaked and frozen. I was as wet and unhappy as everyone else but as I was directing had to try to remain cheerful enough to encourage everyone to keep working so we did not fall behind on our schedule and run into expensive overtime payments. As we prepared for yet another take the actress who was playing the part of the heroine, who had put up with the un-enviable job of lying on a railway line in pouring rain and a bitter wind for most of the day, reminded me that she must leave in thirty minutes to be back in London in time for her evening theatre performance. As the make up artiste did her best to repair the latest rain damage, the actress looked up the line towards the seventy year old steam locomotive which on my cue was to steam towards her and, if all went according to plan, screech to a halt near enough to look from our carefully chosen camera position as it if was right on top of her,

"It will stop, won't it"? she asked me imploringly. I did not have the heart to tell her what the train driver had said to me when I had asked him the same question.

" Well, let's put it this way", he had said puffing at his pipe. "She's an old lady and like all old ladies she has a mind of her own, but if I remember to hit the right levers we should be alright".

I moved back down the line praying silently and cued the action for the umpteenth time. There was no chair with my name on it and no bevy of gorgeous actresses - just a team of dedicated professionals trying to produce good quality results in appalling conditions. The only consolation was that we were all being paid for the work we were doing but that was not the only reason we were there. Like you, we had decided we wanted to follow our chosen ambitions.

## WORKING WITHOUT GLAMOUR

If you are going to work in film or television you should not expect to find you are doing a glamorous job. There is usually plenty of variety but you are likely to find there are also days and possibly months of total boredom. You may be required to work un-social hours. You may find you are working at some exotic location and not have time to enjoy it. The people who produce travel programmes for the television networks often work in places which many would like to visit. When they get home people outside the business usually assume they have been lying on a beach all day and have had a good time. In reality they have often been working from dawn to dusk trying to film a variety of tourist attractions in an absurdly short time. So it is important to ensure that you have the right sort of ambitions and are aware of what you may be letting yourself in for. Then you will like what you are doing enough to take a pride in doing it properly and that is an excellent way to build yourself an interesting career.

A STRANGE WAY TO EARN A LIVING!

WHAT THE AUDIENCE NEVER SEES . . .

SHOOTING AN INTERVIEW.

## AN ESSENTIAL QUALIFICATION

The other essential qualification you must have is an ability to get on with people. If you antagonise others your career is unlikely to prosper. When you make films and videos you are part of a team and one weak link can cause problems for everyone. A few weeks ago I flew into Lisbon with a film crew to shoot scenes for a television report. We arrived just before midnight after a hard day filming in another country and we were all eager to get to bed, but before we could reach our hotel we had to pass through customs with thirteen cases of video equipment. In normal circumstances it is usually a formality because all the equipment is itemised on forms which most customs officers are happy to accept with a minimum of scrutiny. As our flight was the last to arrive there was only one customs officer on duty. He looked as tired as we felt and I had high hopes of being out of the airport in record time. Unfortunately we had a new camera assistant who managed to upset the officer concerned. When he asked to see a lens to check the serial number the assistant rudely told him "It's on the list. Can't you read". It was a stupid remark which immediately caused offence and prompted the officer to check every item we had and demand a complete list of serial numbers. It took us three hours to get out of that airport - three hours which did little to advance the career prospects of one assistant cameraman .

## CONFIRMING YOUR AMBITIONS

When you have answered my preliminary question and are genuinely sure that you want to earn your living in film and television because you are interested in programme making and not because you think it offers a glamorous career, we can proceed to the next stage. Now you know you want to be a programme maker we can start narrow that ambition down even further. You can now try to decide what particular skills

8

you want to acquire and that will help you to define target your final goal in the most effective way.

## HOW TO BE A DIRECTOR

Perhaps you want to be a Director. It's a fine ambition and one you may well be able to achieve but I am going to suggest you should set yourself a less ambitious goal to start with. Like any other senior job it's unusual, and probably unwise, to start at the top even if you can manage to do so. Your ambition may be to direct but your first step should perhaps be to become a competent technician. That may mean starting with a job as a runner or in some relatively junior position. Generally becoming a director is not the starting point for a career. You are more likely to move into the job when you have acquired other skills for you will need those skills when you start to direct. If you do not have them you will be lost and others will soon notice.

Directing a film or video is a very responsible job. You have to be a manager, a co-ordinator and a creator at the same time and steer a balance between commercial and creative considerations. You must satisfy an audience and your financial backers, keep the crew happy and ensure that the final edited version is interesting to watch. When scenes are being filmed you must decide which takes are best and you must ensure that all the different scenes, which will probably not be shot in script order, can eventually be cut together. You will need to have a clear of view what every scene involves and enough technical knowledge to ensure that vision can be turned into reality. It will not be easy. You will encounter thousands of unexpected problems from equipment which breaks down to actors who cannot eat any more ice cream on the 25th take. You will need immense patience and a thorough knowledge of what everyone under your direction is doing. When you are learning the business you will probably find yourself doing many of those jobs yourself and that is an excellent way of preparing yourself to meet your ultimate ambition. You don't have to start at the top to make money or to enjoy yourself.

## OTHER KEY JOBS

Let's spend a few minutes looking at some of the other important jobs people do when they are making films or tv programmes. Perhaps they are jobs you ought to consider. Do you want to be a cameraman? Does recording sound or mixing soundtracks together appeal to you, or are you an editor at heart ? It may help you to decide if we consider what those jobs involve.

## WORKING AS A CAMERAMAN

If you are a cameraman you will be responsible for shooting on film or on video either in a studio or on location. You will need to know all about photography and understand the equipment you have to use. You may need to travel. If you decide to become a news cameraman you are likely to spend much of your life in the air or on the road. If you are a studio based video camerman you may find you are shooting dramas or quiz shows in a studio complex. Every amateur movie maker thinks he or she is a cameraman but doing the job to professional standards is a skilled occupation. You will need to know all about exposure, lighting, filters and the film or video stock you are using and you will find you are often expected to produce professional quality results in conditions which are far from perfect. It can be a very rewarding job and good cameramen can make a lot of money. More importantly it is a fascinating job which can be immensely creative. You should not expect to start your career as a full cameraman. You should normally expect to start as a trainee assistant or perhaps as an assistant if you are working with a small unit. To be a good stills photographer you need a sense of framing and timing. To be a good movie cameraman you will find the same talents helpful but you will need many more. Some can be acquired by reading the right books. The rest must be learned in practice and in this book you will find information which should help you to take your first steps. Camera assistants spend most of their time loading film magazines, pulling focus, labelling film cans or cassette boxes and keeping a record of each scene and take. You may feel that sort of work is unimportant. If that's your view, think again. As I said before, making movies depends on team-work and the success of every team is equally dependent on its most junior member. If you are working as a clapper loader ( another name for a junior camera assistant) and load film incorrectly in a camera magazine, a whole day's filming may be wasted. If you unload film and accidentally fog it or leave a video cassette on top of a radiator, the efforts of everyone else involved may be wasted. Even as a junior member of the production team your contribution will be important. As a Camera assistant you will find you are in an excellent place to learn all about professional film or video photography and that will give you many hours of fascination.

## LIFE AS A SOUND RECORDIST

If you are interested in music or in any sort of tape recording you may find a career in the sound department will satisfy your ambitions. Again you can make money in a number of different ways. Location sound recordists working with film crews record sound on portable tape recorders which are locked to a film camera by a synchronising pulse. Those tapes are then re-recorded on perforated magnetic film and synchronised to the picture by the film editor. When the editor has completed his work he will have an edited reel or reels of picture and a number of different tracks of sound all recorded on perforated magnetic film and edited to match the picture. He will then go into a sound dubbing theatre where another member of the sound department team - the dubbing mixer, will mix them together to produce the final mix which audiences know simply as the soundtrack.

If you want to be a location sound recordist you will need to know all about the different types of microphones so you can record anything from an interview to a full symphony orchestra. You will have to learn how to position microphones to obtain the best quality sound without their interfering with the camera. If microphones are visible when they should be hidden or boom shadows appear on the background or across an artistes face as he or she moves across a set you will not be popular. To become a sound recordist you will again find there are plenty of skills to master. Well recorded sounds can do a great deal to bring a film or video to life and there can be a lot of satisfaction in getting a "clean" recording without background distractions or imperfections of any kind. If you are recording for a video production the sounds you record will probably be recorded directly on to videotape alongside the picture rather than on a separate audio recorder. Again a final soundtrack will be produced by blending a number of tracks together when cutting has been completed. The principle is the same as in film dubbing but there are a number of practical differences as we will see later in this book.

## A DEAD END JOB ?

Some people feel that sound recording is a dead end job. They point to the fact that very few (if any) people move from being sound recordists to being directors and that is certainly true. If you want to become a director you will find the skills you will learn as an editor or a cameraman will probably stand you in better stead but don't let that put you off sound recording if you have a real interest in audio work. Being a professional recordist is a important and creative job and every production needs people who are thoroughly proficient in all the different skills involved. Mixing sounds in dubbing is equally skilled and both jobs offer many creative opportunities as well as a chance to earn a good living.

**THE IMPORTANCE OF EDITING**

One of the most interesting and important jobs in any production team is that of the editor. He or she is responsible for the shape and pace of the finished film or tv programme. A good editor can often bring a relatively dull subject to life by skilful cutting, providing he has suitable pictures and sounds to work with. An uninspired editor can equally easily waste the skills of all the others involved. If well photographed pictures and efficiently recorded sounds are put together inefficiently the finished production may be boring to watch and tedious to hear. A good director should be able to ensure that the editor has suitable materials to work with and does an efficient job but it is also true that a really good editor can be of immense help to an inexperienced director. I can recall hundreds of tv programmes which have been filmed under the direction of people who are experts on the subjects being filmed but not so expert in the techniques of putting them across using an audio visual medium. Editing is one of the most fascinating jobs you can ever hope to do.

**VIDEO EDITING**

On video, as we will see latter, an editor may be required to work "off-line" dealing with a low quality copy of the original material which is later matched electronically to the master. Alternatively he or she may work directly "on line" dealing with the original from the outset. The principal responsibilities for any editor working on film or on tape are to get scenes in the appropriate order and then cut them to length and for effect. A soundtrack must then be edited to match the picture. Perhaps that all sounds very simple. I can assure you it is not. It involves many different tasks most of which offer tremendous creative opportunities. In a later chapter we will see exactly what is involved. At this point it is simply worth bearing in mind that working as an editor you will again be able to make money and enjoy considerable job satisfaction. And if you do want to move on and direct, you will find editing teaches you the importance of good continuity and shows you what you need in terms of sounds and pictures to make a film or video interesting to watch. Many of our most successful film and television directors started their careers in the cutting rooms.

## A DIVERSE INDUSTRY

The jobs we have so far considered are to be found in various branches of the film and television industry. You may find it helpful if we consider how that industry is made up. I have referred to it an one industry but I suppose to be completely accurate I should say indus*tries* for the film industry is really a business on its own. So is television. Video production is another self contained arm and then there are cable and satellite companies to consider. I shall continue to refer to all these inter-connected activities as one industry because they collectively offer you a similar choice of jobs but let's spend a few moments studying each area in a little more detail.

## FEATURE FILMING

Let's start with film. If you want to make films there are several areas you can work in depending on what sort of films interest you most. There's the feature film industry making films for cinema showing and eventually for television release. Many films are also produced by television companies and by independent producers for tv showing and for release on video cassette. If features are your main interest I should warn you now that you will find the going tough. Very few feature films are made each year because of the tremendous costs involved and there are thus relatively few job opportunities. It is a very difficult world to get into even if you are experienced and well qualified. Some have no wish to enter it at all. I have spend my life making films for television and other outlets and have no wish whatever to be involved in making a feature. If you are determined to make feature films but have no professional film production experience, you will need to go to one of the few good film schools with a track record of producing people who have managed to get into that particular world and make a career for themselves. You could almost count their number on one hand. If you want a regular income you are going to find it easier to work in one of the other branches of the industry.

## MAKING DOCUMENTARIES & TV PROGRAMMES

There are far more companies making documentaries and other shorter films and videos for tv showing and for sale or hire on video cassettes. Documentaries vary in style from investigative news reports to productions presenting a corporate image of a company of promoting a product or service to a carefully defined audience. This type of work will probably offer you the best career prospects either as an employee of a tv network or an independent production company. It may also prove to be the easiest to get into.

## PRODUCING CINEMA & TV COMMERCIALS

Making tv and cinema commercials also enables quite a lot of film and television technicians to earn a living. Commercials are normally produced for a sponsor either by an in-house advertising agency production team or by an outside contractor working in association with an agency. The client then buys time on television or in cinemas to show the finished production. It can take several months to make one thirty second commercial with a great deal of planning and argument preceding the actual shooting. There are opportunities in this type of work but long term career prospects are few and far between. You can join an agency and work with their production team or try to persuade an independent company specialising in commercials to take you on their pay-roll. Again you are likely to find they want people with experience of this kind of work. It is certainly lucrative but you may find it hard to get secure long term employment. I personally find there is also a limit on the amount of enthusiasm I can put into promoting a shampoo or trying to convince housewives that a detergent now being sold in a different colour box is significantly better than the old product they were told was so wonderful a few weeks ago.

## TV NETWORKS AND INDEPENDENT PRODUCTION COMPANIES

Television companies and independent production companies will offer you the most opportunities. Because they make so many programmes they need a lot of people and because the programmes they produce are so varied it is likely the work they undertake will be interesting too. At a time when companies are generally laying off staff it may be difficult to find any organisation willing to offer you a permanent staff contract but, with plenty of persistence and adequate proof of your skills and knowledge, you will find that opportunities to work on at least one production still exist. If you do a good job you may be asked to stay on and work on something else. There is an old saying in the industry that you are only as good as your last job and many feel it is true.

## WORKING FREELANCE

When you have acquired the necessary knowledge and experience you can always work on your own or with  friends by going "freelance". Most features are made by freelance technicians because very few big studios  keep permanent production teams. Many television programmes are also bought in by the networks having been made either on commission or independently by outside companies or by freelance technicians. You can even start your own company and in a later chapter we will see what that involves.

So, in all branches of film and television there are people earning their livings doing the sort of jobs you want to do. But how can you join them and make that money you are so keen to earn ? Let's consider the various possibilities.

## BACK TO SCHOOL ?

Before you can get a job you will need to acquire enough skills to encourage someone to employ you. So, what is the best way of acquiring those talents ? You may perhaps think that the easiest way to learn anything new is to go back to school and there are plenty of film schools which will welcome you with open arms, but are they really going to help you ?  There are many sceptics in the industry who feel film school of any kind are a waste of time. There are also others who believe that they can give you a basic knowledge you will find difficult to acquire anywhere else. In my opinion both those opinions are valid. It depends on the school concerned.

## WASTING THREE YEARS ?

Many film schools are under-funded and some operate on such a tight budget that they are not worth considering. It is sad to report that there are also a significant number or organisations which set out to make a profit from their students and from government grants paid to cover their studies. You need to be very careful choosing which school you go to. The first thing to check is the syllabus. How long is the course and what does it cover? You will find some schools allocate up to a year to deal with film history and theory - points which in my view are going to do very little to help you get a job at the end of your studies.

Good schools will concentrate on practical matters and they will have up to date equipment which you can use. If the equipment is old it will probably work badly and will not prepare you for the type of machines you are likely to encounter when you start work. So, check the prospectus carefully and make sure you are not going to be wasting your time. Make sure plenty of time is devoted to practical sessions and adequate opportunities are given for you to work with modern cameras and in a properly equipped cutting room. How many videos or films are you allowed to make in a year and what budget will you be allocated to work with ? Will there be enough to buy sufficient film or tape stock or is so little money available that any practical experiments will have to done on a shoestring budget ? It is also worth checking on the qualifications of the lecturers. Are they people who are currently working in the industry and have plenty of up to date knowledge and experience or just technicians who have taken a job teaching because they are unable to find any other work? Good schools like the National Film School in Britain and the University of South California have a fine track record of doing excellent work but there are others which are principally eager to take your money, so beware ! The American Film Institute publishes a useful list of colleges running courses in film and tv across the United States.

## CHECKING SCHOOLS TRACK RECORDS

There is another point it pays to check before you apply to join any school or college. Find out what has happened to students who have recently completed their courses and try to contact them. There are some schools which are very happy to take your money and lose all interest when you have completed your studies. A badly run course or one which concentrates on things which are unlikely to interest employers will be a waste of time and a waste of money. So,find out if other people have found the course you are considering has helped them to get a job. Have they found it has helped them to acquire skills which they are now using to do a paid job or has it simply given them a certificate or a useless bit of paper? I have encountered many students who have graduated with a degree in audio visual studies or some other equally grand sounding qualification. Only a handful have had enough practical knowledge to be worth considering as potential employees and many were completely useless. They would have done much better to spend a shorter time with a film or video company working in some menial role. They would then have been able to observe what was going on and get a feel for the commercial world in which they were keen to earn a living.

## WORK EXPERIENCE

Another way of getting a foot in the door is to try to persuade an established film or video company to let you work as a runner or simply to watch their staff at work, possibly without even being paid a salary. In my view you are likely to learn more sitting with a good cameraman or an experienced editor for a few days than you are in several months of a college course. If time and funds permit it's a good idea to combine the two. Don't expect any company to be overjoyed at the prospect of your joining them. Most will say "no" and you will find you have to be very persistent if you want to get anywhere. There is no easy way into film or television. The industry is already overmanned and you will find it is extremely difficult to get in but don't be discouraged.

## JOINING A UNION.

When you apply for a job you may be asked if you are a member of a union. A few years ago it was impossible to get any job at all in film or television without a suitable union ticket. In a few areas that situation still exists. The feature film business is particularly union minded but in other areas unions do not wield the power they once had. Many video companies operate without a single union member and even the big television companies are not as militant as they once were. You will find it is quite difficult to get a union ticket. The old farce of not being able to get a job without a ticket and not being able to get a ticket without a job still applies in a few places but fortunately common sense has triumphed in many others.

Unions are not keen to issue new tickets simply because they have so many unemployed members already on their books. If you find it is essential to get a ticket you can apply to the appropriate trade union but the response you get may well be "no", unless you can prove you have a skill which no existing member who is currently unemployed possesses. Working in a film laboratory or a video facilities house can sometimes short circuit "the usual channels". If you speak a foreign language and have to work on a film or tape being produced or dubbed in that language you may also be able to persuade the union that you have qualifications no one on their books possesses. Getting a ticket will probably take time and it is unlikely to be easy but again, don't lose heart. You will encounter plenty of obstacles trying to get into the industry but if you persist and go about it the right way with you will eventually find that somewhere a door will open.

## GETTING THE RIGHT QUALIFICATIONS

Apart from a union ticket, which may or may not be necessary, what qualifications are you going to need to open the doors you need to pass through to start your career in film or television ? As with all jobs, a degree and good exam results will help but if you have failed almost everything at school don't let that put you off. A degree and plenty of good exam passes simply tells a potential employer that you have a brain and are capable of absorbing a reasonable amount of knowledge. If you are practical but not particularly academic you may do equally well in the movie business but you are going to have to convince potential employers that you are their best bet. You can do that in several different ways.

## SELLING YOUR TALENTS

For a minute imagine you are an employer. You are besieged by people wanting jobs and then someone like you comes along. What is your reaction? Are you likely to be impressed ? If you have had an education which has enabled you to read and write without too many mis-spellings you will be off to a good start. If you look smart and are obviously keen to learn you will do even better. If you turn up for an interview looking tatty and behave as if the world owes you a living you will not get far. Your biggest challenge is going to be convincing your first employer that you are worth taking on. He or she will not be easy to convince for your enquiry is unlikely to be the first. If you are going to succeed you have got to put up a very convincing case. You will need to show that you really are interested in the sort of work you are asking to do and it is unlikely to be enough simply to express your interest in words. Enthusiasm certainly helps but potential employers will be looking for hard evidence . They will want to know what you have already done to pursue your ambition.

## PROOF OF INTERESTS AND AMBITIONS

If you are trying to get a job as a cameraman a portfolio of stills may help but it will be better if you can show a video you have shot. When I applied for my first interview you will recall that I sent in a film I had made. It played a major part in getting me my first job and I would definitely recommend you to do the same. It will not be easy. Like me at that time, you will probably not have any professional film equipment and funds may be low. I borrowed a clockwork movie camera (an old Bolex H16) which did not even have a reflex view-finder. I took a temporary job teaching languages at a boys school to get enough money to buy film stock and chose a simple subject which I felt I could do justice to with very limited resources. I decided to make my film about the work on an artist who had pioneered a new technique for glass engraving. He was an extremely talented New Zealander - a man called John Hutton. I first heard of him when he won a big commission to produce one of the main windows in Coventry cathedral which at that time as being rebuilt after being bombed in the war. I was 19 years old with no money or resources. He was already well established and all the big tv companies had done news items on his latest commission. When I first wrote to him I explained that I was very inexperienced but keen to try to do a short film on his work. I did not think he would be interested in working with anyone as inept and inexperienced as me but to my surprise he agreed to see me. I put my cards on the table and told him that I had absolutely nothing but enthusiasm to offer and could not afford to pay him in any way. He asked me what I wanted to do and told me about his approach to art. As he talked and I listened I soon realised I was in the presence of a very interesting man. If only I could get that across on film. He kindly agreed to let me shoot in his studio for two days and gave me a list of completed works. I shot the film on my days off from teaching and in the school holidays hired a professional cutting room for a few days to put the results together. It wasn't a masterpiece but much to my surprise it did later win a film festival award.

The most important thing it did for me was to help be get a job, and for that reason I would thoroughly recommend you to make a showreel yourself. You will find that when you are making it you learn a great deal and you are also likely to have plenty of fun. A showreel will do more than anything else to help you to find a way into film and television and in the following chapters we are going to see how you can produce it.

# CHAPTER TWO
# PLANNING YOUR SHOWREEL

## WHO PAYS ?

Who is going to pay for your showeeel ? Are you going to meet the costs yourself or will your family be asked to contribute ? Do you intend to try to find a commercial sponsor or will you borrow the money from a bank ? Those are the next questions you must ask yourself. You may be able to find organisations which will be prepared to assist you with a grant if the subject you are intending to film suits their objectives. Books like the Whole Film Source Book (Published by Universe Books, New American Library New York in 1983) may help to put you in touch with organisations which can offer grants for specific projects. In the USA, federal government funds may be available and in the UK organisations like the Arts Council and the Greater London Arts Association may sometimes contribute towards the cost of films and videos on arts subjects. If you are unable to find anyone to help you will have to finance production yourself or find a commercial sponsor.

## BORROWING FROM A BANK

If your bank balance is low you may be able to persuade your bank manager to give you an overdraft or a business development loan. In either case he or she may want some form of security and the interest charges are likely to be high. Banks are not very keen on investing in unknown quantities and until you have your first commercial success as a film or video maker or manage to find a regular job paying you a reasonable salary, from a banker's point of view your are a bad risk. So, while it may be worth talking to your bank, you may find it is difficult to negotiate a loan on satisfactory terms. Before you approach a bank you will need to prepare a detailed estimate of the costs you expect to incur and an outline of what you are proposing to do. They will also want to know how you propose to recover your money and repay their loan. Make your proposals look as professional as possible. Later in this chapter we will consider the costs you need to assess and see how you can go about it. If your bank will not help you and you do not have any money yourself, you may be forced to do what I did and take a temporary job to raise some cash. While you are doing that job you can spend your spare time planning your showreel and the more time you devote to it even at this early stage, the better the end result is likely to be.

## CHOOSING THE RIGHT SUBJECT

The most important decision you have to make is your choice of subject. The main purpose of your showreel is to demonstrate your talents and to help you acquire them while it is being made but, like all film and video productions, your ultimate aim must be to interest and entertain an audience. If you produce something which is boring to watch or difficult to follow it will do little to advance your career prospects. Your choice will probably be limited by the your budget. If you have unlimited funds you could choose an ambitious subject but for a first production I would strongly recommend you to opt for something simple. Pick a subject which interests you and one you feel you can do justice to. When I decided to make my showreel I considered a lot of different subjects. I eventually decided to explore the work and views of an artist for several reasons. Artists are creative and they usually have something interesting to say and to show. I had very little money so filming anything which needed actors or numerous locations was out of the question. In any case I had no experience of working with actors and almost no technical knowledge so I would have made a complete mess of anything ambitious. I realize that now but then I was not fully aware of all the implications of my inexperience. The decision was finally made when I sat down and tried to work out a budget. I calculated how many days I was going to need to hire equipment for and how much travelling and overnight accommodation I would have to pay for visiting all the locations at which I needed to film. By professional standards the total added up to a sum which could have been met out of petty cash but to me, at that time trying to start a career without any money, it seemed a fortune. You may be in the same situation. If you are, I would strongly advise you to choose a simple subject which you can do justice to without stretching your resources or spending the rest if your life in debt to a bank. Keep it simple and do not try to do everything at once. Take your time and you will avoid a lot of unnecessary problems.

**BEING TOO AMBITIOUS**

Even the simplest subject can be interesting to film if you go about it the right way. I once set some students an exercise which I knew they would loathe just to see what sort of results they could produce. They were about to make their first video - a 5 minute practical exercise intended to give them a first taste of "hands on" work. When they were asked to suggest subjects they would like to film, some came up with quite practical ideas. Others produced suggestions which were far too ambitious. One outlined a script which needed a cast of fifteen actors and had a story set in the 16th century. All very commendable later in life but not very practical on a shoestring budget which would not even cover the hire of the costumes. Making films and videos is principally a business and it is important to realize that costs must be related to what one hopes the eventual return will be.

## A TALENT SPOTTING EXERCISE

The subject those students were asked to film was deliberately chosen to see how creative and intelligent they could be when faced with a topic which had no obvious charm, or creative merit. I asked them to make a video telling audiences how to fit an electric plug to a portable heater. Try to bring a subject as dull as that to life and you will find you are facing a considerable challenge! The students had two weeks to produce their videos. Most of them produced tapes which were adequately shot and they opted for the obvious treatment. They simply set up a camera and filmed someone putting on a plug , shot from one camera position and then inter-cut those shots with a Presenter talking to camera, explaining the correct procedure step by step. It was adequate but not very interesting to watch. When the videos were shot the students soon found that the subject was not as straightforward as it at first seemed. The people who were asked to appear in the videos and actually fit the plugs almost all had trouble doing it neatly and safely first time. They cut wires to the wrong length, lost their grip on the fuses and generally made a mess of take after take. In the worst tapes, where problems had occurred they were simply edited out and the action jumped when they started again. In the more professional tapes, cutaways (see page 117) had been inserted so when something went wrong we were shown a quick shot of the face of the person fitting the plug before a retake of their hands came on the screen. Continuity was thus preserved and those videos were a little more pleasant to watch. Imaginative titles set other videos apart from those which were totally run of the mill but one particular tape stood head and shoulders above the rest.

## MAKING A DULL SUBJECT INTERESTING

The student who made the best tape of all used the same equipment and resources as everyone else. The only difference in his approach and that followed by most of the others was that he used his imagination. He considered the subject and decided to expand the obvious treatment just enough to give his video an interesting start and end. What, he had thought, happens when someone fits a plug the wrong way? He went to talk to some local safety experts and soon discovered that if the wires were fitted the wrong way round it could start a fire. He continued with his research using libraries and visiting fire fighting experts and managed to find stills of a house which had been burned to the ground after a fire started by an electrical fault. He then went out and bought a plug identical to the one mentioned in the fire investigators report. He tampered with it and set it on fire until it looked like the one which had caused all the trouble and then he started to make his video.

It began with shots of firefighters racing along a street to the scene of a fire. That shot dissolved into flames and the flames then gave way to a photograph of that fire blackened house. The flame shot was obtained by filming a sheet of burning paper very close up and mixing slowly into the still. Sounds of alarm bells and fire crackle were added and the video began in a spectacular way which immediately won audiences' interest. He then introduced his subject with a few well chosen words. I cannot remember exactly what they were but it was something along the following lines·

" When fire breaks out the cost can be high. In this house a family died in four minutes, and the cause was as simple as this".

We then saw the burned out plug and the video's opening titles were superimposed. The tape then went on to show what was wrong with the plug which strated the fire and how it should have been fitted. The message was presented in a clear way which was easy to follow. The student carefully selected the angles from which he filmed every one of his shots. It was a thoroughly professional job and one which showed that even the more boring subject can be made interesting if you go about it the right way.

## FINDING A SPONSOR

So what subject are *you* going to choose? I am sure you are not going to show us how to fit a plug but I hope you are equally unlikely to want to try to remake the latest science fiction epic. Keep it simple and you will enjoy it more and the end result can still be impressive. If you are looking for funds you may be able to find a subject which a commercial sponsor will be prepared to invest in. It is no use approaching a multi- national firm which has a large budget for films and videos and telling them you want to make their next production. Even if they were daft enough to give you the commission, you would soon be in trouble because at this stage, without enough experience you would not be able to meet the standards they require. If you decide to approach any commercial concern you need to be completely honest. Tell them that you are new to the business and are trying to get experience. A good company will not hold that against you and indeed should appreciate your honesty. If you try to pull the wool over their eyes and pretend things are not as they are, they will quickly see through you and will not be impressed.

If you are trying to attract the interest of a sponsor you will find it pays to suggest a subject which they can benefit from. It may be something to do with their line of business. Perhaps they are sponsoring a local carnival and would like a video record of it. Alternatively you may be able to suggest a subject which they are not directly connected with but will not mind having their name linked to - perhaps a local charity which does a lot of good work and which the commercial sponsor might be happy to be seen to be helping. Alternatively you could approach a local charity yourself. Charities, unlike some international concerns, are usually short of money and often cannot afford to sponsor a full scale production made by a well established company but if you can produce worthwhile results on a limited budget they may be interested. Again be honest. Tell them what you have or have not done and what you would like to do for them. Get your ideas worked out before you approach them. Find out all about their activities and if they interest you and you feel you can do justice to them, work out what you would need to film to do the job properly. You can then work out what it will cost to shoot on film or video. You can then try to see whoever is in charge of that particular organisation. Tell them what you know of their work so they know you have taken the trouble to find out about what they are doing. You can then explain why you think you can help them, by getting their activities some more publicity and giving them a video they can use to show what they are doing and raise more funds.

**SELLING IDEAS TO SPONSORS**

When you are selling ideas it is always worth trying to present them from your customers point of view. In this case ask yourself what the charity's problems are. They may have some new project in mind - perhaps an extension to an old peoples day centre or an additional kidney machine. You can then make your video sound like a more attractive proposition by pointing out that it could be used to help to raise funds for that particular project. The treatment will need to be carefully planned so it covers all the right points, but if you work with your potential sponsor and are honest throughout you could find you establish a good partnership from which you can both benefit.

When you have found a subject which appeals to you and one which it is going to be practicable to explore with the resources you have, you and, if you have one, your sponsor will want to know how much your film or video is going to cost. Your next job will be working that out and before you can do that you must make some more important decisions.

## FILM OR VIDEO ?

You can make your showreel on film or video. That's your first choice but it isn't quite a simple as it sounds. There are a number of different formats. Some are more expensive than others . If you opt for one it may cost you twice as much as another. And there are other considerations too depending on the type of audience you want to reach and the ways in which you intend to show your completed production. Let's consider each of these points.

## WORKING ON FILM

If you decide to shoot on film it does not mean you will only be able to show your completed film in cinemas or on a film projector. As you  probably already know, films can be recorded on videotape perfectly satisfactorily if the appropriate technical points are considered. So, why not shoot everything on film and forget about tape altogether until the final stage ? There are people who feel the quality of film is superior to anything any video format has to offer and for some types of showing they are right. If you want to show your showreel in a cinema on a giant screen or produce versions for use in third world countries, where video machines are not widely available, film is undoubtedly the medium to use. If money is no object it is also a very creative format to adopt. There are two main film sizes to choose from. 35mm film is the size used for making films for cinema showings. Film is measured and bought in feet. A thousand feet of 35mm film runs for around ten minutes. Film stock is expensive and so is processing but the quality can be superb. 16mm film is cheaper and still widely used in television. 400ft of 16mm film runs for around ten minutes. Again you will have to met the cost of buying unexposed film, processing it and preparing a copy for editing. You will also incur the costs of making show prints and safety copies. If you work on videotape your costs will be lower.

## VIDEO STANDARDS

In video, as with film, you will have to choose between several different systems. As you have no doubt already discovered, there are a number of different kinds of videotape. Around the world you will encounter various systems and formats. The most popular ones are :

*Systems* : PAL   NTSC   SECAM

*Broadcast quality Formats* : 1 Inch. Betacam SP
High Band Umatic

*Domestic Quality Formats* : VHS. Betamax .Video 8/ Hi8
Low Band U-Matic

Your choice of system will be quite straightforward. It will largely depend on where you live and where your showreel is going to be produced. The three different systems I have listed are used in different areas of the world because, when video was first introduced, the major powers were unable to agree on a common system. The British went their way and adopted a system known as PAL . The letters stand for Phase Alternation Line and PAL equipment is used in Britain, most commonwealth countries and many others in Europe. NTSC (National Television Systems Committee) is the system used in the USA and most American influenced states. SECAM (Sequentiel Couleur a Memoire) is the French tv system which is also used in Russia. It is quite possible to convert recordings made on one system to play on another. There is a noticeable loss of quality but it is done all the time, as you can see every day if you watch television news. You should choose to work on the system which is most widely used where you intend to shoot and edit your production. If you subsequently need copies in another format for showing elsewhere that can be dealt with when the needs arises. Here is a guide to the systems principally used in various countries. In each instance I have listed the system most widely used but it will usually prove possible to hire or buy other systems locally if you are prepared to shop around.:

| | | | |
|---|---|---|---|
| ABU DHABI | PAL | ALGERIA | PAL |
| AUSTRALIA | PAL | ANGOLA | PAL |
| AUSTRIA | PAL | ARGENTINA | PAL |
| BAHAMAS | NTSC | BAHRAIN | PAL |
| BANGLADESH | PAL | BARBADOS | NTSC |
| BELGIUM | PAL | BERMUDA | NTSC |
| BOTSWANA | PAL | BRAZIL | PAL |
| BRUNEI | PAL | BULGARIA | SECAM /PAL |
| CANARY ISLANDS | PAL | CAYMAN ISLE | NTSC |
| CHILE | NTSC | CHINA | PAL |
| COLUMBIA | NTSC | COSTA RICA | NTSC |
| CUBA | NTSC | CYPRUS | PAL/ SECAM |
| CZECKOSLOVAKIA | SECAM | DENMARK | PAL |
| DUBAI | PAL | EGYPT | SECAM |
| FINLAND | PAL | FRANCE | SECAM |
| GERMANY | PAL/ SECAM | GREECE | SECAM |
| GREENLAND | NTSC | HATI | SECAM |
| HAWAII | NTSC | HONG KONG | PAL |

| | | | |
|---|---|---|---|
| HUNGARY | SECAM | ICELAND | PAL |
| INDIA | PAL | INDONESIA | PAL |
| IRAN | SECAM /PAL | IRAQ | SECAM |
| IRELAND | PAL | ISRAEL | PAL |
| ITALY | PAL | JAPAN | NTSC |
| JORDAN | PAL | KENYA | PAL |
| KOREA | NTSC | KUWAIT | PAL |
| LIBYA | PAL | MADERIA | PAL |
| MALAYSIA | PAL | MALTA | PAL |
| MEXICO | NTSC | MONACO | SECAM |
| MOZAMBIQUE | PAL | NETHERLANDS | PAL |
| NEW ZEALAND | PAL | NIGERIA | PAL |
| NORWAY | PAL | OMAN | PAL |
| PAKISTAN | PAL | PANAMA | NTSC |
| PHILLIPINES | NTSC | PORTUGAL | PAL |
| PUERTO RICO | NTSC | SINGAPORE | PAL |
| SAUDI ARABIA | SECAM/PAL | SOUTH AFRICA | PAL |
| SPAIN | PAL | SRI LANKA | PAL |
| SWEDEN | PAL | SWITZERLAND | PAL |
| SYRIA | SECAM | THAILAND | PAL |
| TOBAGO & TRINIDAD | NTSC | TUNISIA | SECAM |
| UGANDA | PAL | ARAB EMIRATES | PAL |
| UNITED KINGDOM | PAL | USA | NTSC |
| USSR | SECAM | VATICAN | PAL |
| VENEZUELA | NTSC | ZAMBIA | PAL |

## CHOOSING THE RIGHT FORMAT

If choosing the system you are going to use is fairly straightforward, selecting the format you are going to adopt is going to require more consideration. You are probably already familiar with formats like VHS ( video home system) and indeed you may wonder why it is worth giving the subject any more thought. You have a VHS recorder at home and own or can borrow a VHS camera. Why not make your showreel on that and forget about everything else ? You can certainly do that but it is not a course I would recommend for the following reasons.

## PUTTING QUALITY FIRST

VHS is intended for home use. It is a half inch cassette format developed by the JVC company and intended principally for home movie making and the recording of television programmes at home for family viewing. It is fine for the purpose for which it was developed but the tape speed and signal strength are nowhere near as good as tapes recorded on more elaborate equipment designed to produce results of broadcast television quality. As a result when a VHS tape is copied it loses more quality than a tape recorded on a broadcast quality system. You have probably seen home movies which have been shot on equipment intended for domestic use. The original looks sharp and the colours are good. The first copy looks fuzzier and the sound has a slight hiss. Duplicate that copy again and the results will begin to look rough. Picture definition will deteriorate even more and the sound will suffer too. In the course of making any professional production - and that includes your showreel - you are inevitably going to need to copy the original tape several times in the course of editing and dubbing. You will then probably need to make another duplicate tape to safeguard your original when you are producing copies. If the tape and system you shoot your programme on is designed to produce images and sounds of broadcast quality as opposed to results intended for home use, you should not have a problem. You will start with a tape with a picture definition of at least 700 lines. Your copies, up to two or three generations away from the master, will look much the same as the original and only when you reach four or five stages will any change be noticed by the average viewer. If you work on a digital system the different generations will be almost impossible to spot. So, it is worth deciding to work on a broadcast quality system. You will then have a good quality original which will remain agreeable to look at an pleasant to hear as work progresses and do you credit when audiences see the end result. In practice that means you will probably decide to master your programme on either a one inch or a Betacam SP tape.

## ONE INCH TAPE AND BETACAM SP

Until recently most major television networks used one inch tape machines for all their recordings. The machines are bulky, tape reels are expensive and they take up too much space, but quality is superb. Nowadays technical advances have made it possible to obtain excellent quality from more compact formats. There are a number in use but the most widely used is probably Betacam SP made by Sony. I have used it for many years and have a component SP cutting room installed in my home so I can keep an eye on the quality of the various productions I am involved in. It's a system I can thoroughly recommend and, as this book progresses, we will see what is involved in making your showreel on BETA SP and on film at every stage. If you decide to choose some other format the advice I will be giving can easily be adapted to suit other formats. The important decision is the first one you will have to make. Do you go for a home based system or for broadcast quality ? You have already heard some arguments which may help you to make up your mind and here are some others you may care to consider.

## PAYING FOR QUALITY

Home video systems - like VHS - are deliberately priced to attract home movie makers. We have already considered their advantages and drawbacks but we have not really explored the price difference. It is considerable. If a domestic video unit costs you the financial equivalent of 500 units, a Betacam SP recorder could cost you up to thirty times as much. As this book is going to be read internationally I intend to give my guide prices in units rather than in one of many ever fluctuating currencies,but if you convert those units into your local currency you will get a good idea of the enormous difference between the two prices. But don't forget that crucial word *quality!*

You may now be wondering if I have gone out of my mind. There are you, going to make a showreel on limited resources, and here am I telling you it's in your own interests to use equipment which would cost an experienced technician many years salary. Don't worry. You do not need to raise that kind of money. You can hire the equipment you require when you need it. You do not have to buy it.

**GOOD QUALITY ON A TIGHT BUDGET**

When you have decided which system you intend to use you can choose what camera you want to hire and what days you want to use it on. You can also hire a fully equipped broadcast quality edit suite or a film cutting room either with or without an editor. As this book progresses we will be looking at both these options in depth. So don't let cost factors deflect you from a concern for quality. It's the quality of your final edited version which counts in the end.

**OTHER VIDEO FORMATS**

You will have noticed that I mentioned four formats which we have not so far explored. They were Betamax, Video/Hi 8 and high and low band U-Matic. What are they all about ? Betamax is principally another home movie system. It was quite popular in the USA but never really caught on in Europe, largely because the video rental firms decided to adopt VHS. The quality of Betamax recordings is good. Many feel it is significantly better than VHS but it is still a system which is not intended to produce broadcast quality results. If you copy Betamax tapes you will find you have a similar problem to the one I have discussed above. You will not retain the same image quality as you will if you start with a broadcast quality original. Beta*max* should not be confused with Beta*cam* SP. That is a broadcast quality system. The tape runs at a different speed through a totally different system. The results are superb and high quality can be sustained for several generations.

## MIXING FORMATS

Hi 8 and video 8 are also Sony inventions. An eight millimetre tape cassette records good quality pictures and sounds. Though intended principally for domestic home movie use, Hi 8 is used by some professionals. It has been adopted for news purposes by some tv stations because it is extremely portable. For candid under cover filming it has much to recommend it. Hi 8 originals can be transferred (i.e. re-recorded) on to a broadcast quality tape for editing and intercutting with other material. There is some loss of quality and an expert will notice the difference when Hi 8 and Beta SP original shots are intercut but the format is good and it does have its uses. If you have a video 8 camera and want to shoot on that I would not rule it out but I would suggest you should not attempt to do any creative editing on the same format. Use Hi 8 which is significantly better quality than normal 8mm and get your 8mm original transferred to Beta SP before you start cutting. Better still, shoot all your material on a Beta SP camera or on some other broadcast format so you have a superb quality original to work with.

## WORKING ON U-MATIC

That just leaves us with high and low band U-Matic. U-Matic is a Sony trade name for a three quarter inch video format which was very widely used until Betacam became popular and the prices of Betacam systems dropped. U-Matic tapes are still quite commonly used for off line editing. The wider tape and good quality engineering produces better quality than standard VHS. Some people still record their master tapes on U-matic though it is no longer a course I would personally recommend. The quality is not nearly as good as the more expensive broadcast systems and in my view it is worth paying the extra. U-Matic tapes can be used on two different types of recorder. Low band machines use a low frequency recording system which gives a quality which is better than standard VHS but not anything like as good as any broadcast system. High Band Umatic machines use a much higher frequency response and there is a noticeable improvement in quality over anything recorded on a low band equipment. A few years ago, when people wanting to achieve broadcast quality results had to either opt for working on 1 inch masters which were expensive and bulky or on Beta SP which was expensive when it was first introduced, high band U-Matic recording offered a relatively low cost alternative for achieving acceptable results. Many small organisations producing in- house videos or low budget sponsored programmes tended to use U- Matic high band and some still do. Now the cost of better quality systems has fallen I personally feel U-Matic systems can only serve a useful purpose when they are used for off line editing. In my view it is better to shoot your master on film or an optimum quality broadcast video system (like Betacam SP) and then edit either on line, using the master tape, or off line with either a U-Matiic or even a super VHS copy which can later be conformed to match the master recording on the tape originally exposed in the camera.

## SUMMARY

Let's summarise. You can make your showeel more cheaply by working on a home movie system like VHS or Betamax but if you do that the quality of your original tape will deteriorate when you copy it. Your ability to do creative editing will also be severely limited by the equipment which is available. Alternatively you can decide to work on either film or a broadcast video system. The most widely used broadcast system is probably Betacam SP. There are other systems including a Super VHS but they will not offer you the same quality. You do not have to buy the equipment you need to work with. You can hire it when it is required. Alternatively you can work on film, shooting on 35mm film if you are interested in cinema and other large screen showings or on 16mm if you are targeting television or other forms of projection. If you opt for film your production costs are likely to be higher but you can show you finished production on a large screen or on any type of video cassette and expect good quality results. When you have chosen the system you want to use, you can begin to work out what your showreel will cost.

## PRODUCING A BUDGET

When you have chosen the subject you want to film and decided the format you intend to work on you can produce a production budget and find out how much your showreel is likely to cost. You will need to consider a number of items including the following.

*1.Script.*

Are you going to employ a professional scriptwriter or do the job yourself ? If you are using a professional you will need to negotiate a fee for preparing an outline treatment and developing it into a full shooting script. If you are going to do your own work you will still need to allow for material costs like paper and duplicating. If you are going to prepare a fully professional budget you should also assess the time you are going to need and include a rate for that in your budget.

*2.Artistes.*

If you are proposing to film a dramatised script you may need actors. Professional actors are usually paid a fee based on their own standing in the profession, the amount of time they are required for and on where the final edited production will be shown. A film or video intended to television showing will command a higher fee than an educational video being produced for use in a factory or a school. Most artistes have agents who will be happy to negotiate a daily rate. You may also be expected to may an insurance charge and the cost of getting your artistes to and from the location(s) at which filming is to take place. If you are making an advertising commercial you will find many agents will want to negotiate a repeat fee which paid every time the commercial is shown.

If you are not planning to make a programme which requires actors or actresses performing in front of the camera either in a dramatic role or as presenters/anchormen, you may still require a professional artiste to read any voice over narration. *Voice overs,* as they are referred to in the trade, are a lucrative line for artistes. You have no doubt heard many famous actors extolling the virtues of cornflakes or soap powders and there are many lesser known artistes who make a good living entirely doing this kind of work. It is a specialist skill. Not every actor can do it. I have encountered many who, while they are excellent in vision, are unable to command attention throughout a film when they are merely reading the script as a voice over. The cost of any artiste(s) you need for this type of work should be included in your budget. Agents will normally be happy to negotiate a fee per reel based on the running time of the final edited version. If you want a well known name you should expect to pay a higher fee. You will also need to budget for the recording time needed and for the use of a sound recording studio.

*3. Producer/ Directors fees.*

As this is your first production you will possibly be doing much of this work yourself so the costs which normally need to be considered under this heading may not arise. If you are preparing a budget for a commercial sponsor you should include a fee for the time involved in preparing the film/video for production, shooting it and seeing it through editing and the other post production stages. You might even include a bottle of champagne to enjoy when work is complete!

*4. Salaries (Technicians)*

You will need a cameraman and a camera assistant, a sound recordist and possibly a boom operator to assist him or her. You will also need an editor who will probably require an assistant. You may need someone to help with the lighting and a production secretary. Camera and sound crews are normally paid on a daily basis. If a cameraman gets the equivalent of a hundred and fifty units a day you should expect to pay an assistant around a hundred and a sound recordist about the same. You may be able to negotiate an all in rate for the whole job at a total which is lower than the normal daily rate.

When you assess these costs and work out a shooting schedule it is important to consider the possibility of any overtime payments. If you produce an unrealistic shooting schedule or negotiate absurdly low fees you may find you are faced with overtime bills which double the budget. Again the costs covered by this heading may not all be relevant to you making your first showreel but it's not a bad idea to know what is normally involved.

## 5. Sets and locations

You are probably not going to be working in a studio at this stage because the costs involved may be prohibitive, but if you need any specially built sets you should include the cost of making and transporting them in your budget. You may just need a dummy wall or a particular object to hide something you do not want to show. For example, if you are shooting street scenes and your script is set in the 1950s you will not want the audience to see any parking meters. One way of eliminating a meter is to put a dummy post box or a plastic tree over it. The cost of that sort of activity should be included in your budget under this heading.

## 6. Lighting

If you are planning to film indoors you will need lighting. The best plan is to hire what you require by the day or for the duration of the shoot. Specialist film lighting companies will be able to give you a daily rate or an all inclusive one for the duration of your shoot. If you are lighting a small area a portable lighting kit like four redheads (650w bulbs in holders which can be focussed to spot or flood) may well suffice. If you have to light larger areas you will need more and stronger lights. A couple of blondes may be required. Before any of my male readers get excited I should perhaps explain that "blonde" is the term normally used for a 500w lamp. If you have large dark areas to light you will need even larger lights and possibly a generator. With modern film and tape stocks, lighting budgets are nowhere near as expensive as they were when the fastest colour film was 16ASA. In really well lit areas you may be able to work without any lighting at all, but I would personally recommend carrying at least a redhead kit if you are doing any filming indoors. You can use lighting creatively to make your pictures look better than they will look if you try to get by with what is normally available and you can control the depth of your focus more accurately, as we will discover in a later chapter.

*7. Camera Equipment Hire.*

We have already considered lighting so what other items are you likely to require ? You will need a camera with all its accessories. When you hire a film or video camera you will also need a tripod, batteries and various other items. For a film camera you will want to have spare film magazines and a changing bag which can be used to load and unload film when a darkroom is not available. Most equipment hire companies offer a package which includes a camera, a zoom lens, batteries and a limited range of accessories like a tape measure to check the accuracy of your focus. Film cameras are often supplied with a 10 - 1 zoom lens and video cameras with a 14 x 9 zoom. You can always specify the type of lens you require though you should be prepared to pay a higher daily rate for anything other than the standard equipment normally fitted. Telephoto and wide angle lenses can all be hired by the day. If you have a particular location where you need a very wide angle you can economise by only hiring that lens for the day on which you need it and using a standard zoom for the rest of your shoot. Cameras and accessories arc usually supplied in metal carrying cases ready for transit.

If you are shooting on video you may also need to hire extra tv monitors and a playback unit. You can always view what you have shot by rewinding the tape and watching as it is played back in the viewfinder but the picture will be in black and white. It will also be so small it will cannot be used as a guide to quality. I would suggest you should hire at least a colour monitor which can be connected to the output of your camera to give you a colour picture when you are shooting or use in conjunction with a back adaptor to view all the scenes and takes at the end of each day. Again these items can be hired on a daily basis.

*8. Sound equipment hire.*

If you are shooting on video you can record directly on to your videotape master. You will simply have to hire suitable microphones for the sounds you have to record and make sure you have the right cables and connections to feed the signal into the camera. If you are using more than one microphone you may need to hire an audio mixer unit and connect the output of that to your camera. Most broadcast cameras have two microphone inputs. The type of microphone(s) you need will depend on what you are shooting. If you are just recording sound effects a telescopic gun mike like a Sennheiser 416 will probably suffice. Most broadcast cameras have telescopic mikes built in but it is better to use a detachable one with a wind shield so you can place it wherever you wish. If you are proposing to record dialogue you may need personal mikes which can be clipped on to the clothing of those you wish to record. Radio microphones, which will enable you to record good quality sound while the camera is some distance away, can also be useful. They too can be hired by the day.

*9. Wardrobe*

If you are proposing to shoot any period scenes or need policemen or others in special uniforms the cost of hiring those items should be allowed for at an early stage.

Costumiers will give you a daily rate for each item you require. You will need to give them a detailed brief well in advance of your shooting date and you must make sure your brief is very precise. It is no use ringing up a supplier and just saying you want a policeman's uniform on Thursday week. They want to know what area the policeman is supposed to be working in and what year the production is set in. They will also require the head, feet, collar, waist and inside leg measurements of the artiste concerned. If you fail to supply all that information you could find yourself stuck with a Los Angeles policeman in a 1930's uniform when you are shooting shots supposed to be taking place in London in 1995.

*10. Music*

Are you proposing to use any music in your showreel ? If you feel it is needed, you have another choice to make. Are you going to commission specially composed music or will you use recordings which are already available ? If you decide to commission an original work you will need to negotiate a fee with a composer. The costs of writing the music and of recording it will need to be considered. For your first exercise, unless you have friend in a band or with a synthesiser who you feel would be able to do a good job, it is probably best to use recordings which have already been issued.

There are a number of companies which specialize in supplying "mood music" for use in film and tv productions. Their recordings have the advantage that, as they are designed for film use, their copyright is internationally clearable at reasonable cost. If you use a standard commercial recordings bought in a record shop you could find yourself faced with an enormous bill for royalties for the artistes(s) and musician(s). If you use mood disks you will simply be asked to declare the amount of music you have used, specifying the name(s) and number(s) of the disk(s) and the band(s) you have actually recorded. You will then have to pay a royalty fee based on the amount of music used , the type of programme you are making and the territory it is to be shown in. For a showreel intended for internal company use or for private educational showings the fee will be much lower than it will if your production is to be transmitted on TV from coast to coast. If you are lucky enough to sell your programme in more territories than you expect, you can make additional payments when those territories sign a contract. For example, if you are working in Chicago and only intend your video to be shown to potential employers in your area you can make your first declaration and pay the limited fee required for non-theatric use on video in one state. If you subsequently find the video is more successful than you ever envisaged, and manage to sell it for a TV showing in the USA or overseas, you can make a further payment when that sale is concluded and advise the copyright holder (normally the Mechanical Copyright Protection Society or its local equivalent body) of the new deal. For your initial production budget you should assess the amount of music you are likely to need and include a suitable figure.

## 11. Film / Tape stock and processing.

If you are proposing to shoot on film, this could be one of the most expensive items in your budget. If you are shooting on tape the cost of buying the master tapes you require will be minimal. Working on video you will be able to shoot much more at a lower cost. A 30 minute cassette of broadcast quality videotape is likely to cost you less than half the cost of an unexposed roll of colour negative film. When you have shot your tape you can immediately edit the original by dubbing it on to another broadcast quality tape or by working off line with a lower quality copy. Again the cost of the stock will be minimal.

If you shoot on film the camera original will have to be developed and a copy will then need to be printed before editing can begin. The cost of the raw film stock, developing it and printing that first print should be included in your budget. The first copies are known as "rushes" or "dailies" because they are always produced in a hurry, often overnight. In the past it was impossible to see what you had actually filmed until the rushes were screened and every morning key members of the production team would assemble in a preview theatre to see the results of the previous day's shoot. When you are working on film, that still happens but the advent of small video cameras set into film cameras to provide a simultaneous rough video picture of what is being filmed, has meant that no one is now surprised by the results seen on the screen when rushes are projected.

You will also need to budget for the stock used in the final stages of production. Working on tape that simply means another tape cassette for sound dubbing and one more for the final edited version. If you are working on film, when the rushes have been edited and the final format has been determined, that edited copy ( then known not as "dailies" but as the "cutting copy" or "work print") will be returned to the laboratory. The camera original will then be matched to it in an operation known as negative cutting. When every scene has been matched cut for cut, the original can be printed on another new roll of stock to make the first show print It will be free of joins and the colours, which will have been adjusted by a technician known as a *grader* before the cut master is printed, should look as the cameraman intended. Lab costs are a considerable item and one of the main reasons why so many producers have switched from film to tape. The arguments I advanced earlier about working on film for large screen showings should be borne in mind when you assess your budget. Working on film, stock costs will be higher but if you are intent on a cinema or other large screen showing you should take the plunge and include them in your budget. The mains film stock costs are :

*Raw (unexposed) stock.* You should allow for much more stock than the final running time of your film as you will inevitably shoot much more than you ever use in the final edited version. A ratio of 10 - 1 is what many allow for. So if you are planning to end up with a film running for around 10 minutes ( 400ft of 16mm film or 1000 foot of 35mm) you should budget for shooting around 4,000 foot of 16mm film (ten 400ft rolls). For a 35mm film that adds up to 10,000 feet of film.

*Processing the original*

You will also need to include the laboratory cost of developing the camera original, calculated in the footages I have outlined above, and of printing the rushes. That's the same amount of print stock.

*Negative cutting and producing a show print*

Ask the laboratory what they are going to charge to match your edited cutting copy to the camera original and to make a final show print. The length of the show print will be the duration of your finished film, so if it's a ten minute production you only need to allow for the cost of the stock needed to make a ten minute print. In the chapter on editing you will find more information on what is involved.

Working on video you simply need to allow for buying high quality blank videotapes. Again you should expect to shoot far more than you ever expect to use. Filming never goes exactly as planned. It would be wonderful if it did, but you will find however well you plan things, unexpected events occur. Artistes forget their lines. People appear in the background when their presence is not required and equipment fails to work. There are many reasons why you need to allow for the cost of much more stock than your will require to make copies of your final edited programme and that must be borne in mind when you are preparing your budget. I have suggested a shooting ratio of 10 - 1, which is about average for a professional production, but that figure should not be taken as gospel. There are some subjects where you may find you have to shoot much more. Doing interviews with members of the public for example can be a very costly business. To get one sentence you can use you may have to shoot for ten minutes or more. Filming sporting events also tends to use up a lot of stock and when you are making documentaries on subjects where every action you need to portray cannot be precisely scripted and rehearsed in advance, you may well end up shooting more than you would in a studio with professional artistes and a well rehearsed script.

*12 Editing*

When your showreel has been shot, you will have to produce an edited version. As this is your first production you may wish to do the work yourself and in a later chapter you will find comprehensive notes to help you. If you are not particularly interested in editing or feel the task will be beyond you, you will need to enlist the help of an experienced editor. He or she will probably wish to work with an assistant, particularly if you have shot your showreel on film. Most editors will be happy to agree a fee for undertaking all the work involved from the end of shooting to the delivery of your first show copy of the final edited version.

Editing, as I hope you are already aware, involves much more than the popular image of simply cutting out the bad bits.It is a crucial stage of production and you are going to need adequate equipment to do the job properly. If you are working on film it will be best for you to hire a fully equipped cutting room. If you are attempting to edit a 15 minute film you should allow at least three weeks for making the first assembly, developing it into a fine cut version, and then track laying. I am assuming that you are going to leave the final stage of editing - negative cutting - to the laboratory or to an outside contractor specializing in that kind of work. To find out what matching the master to the cutting copy is going to cost tell the laboratory how long you think your final edited film will be and they will give you a price.

If you are working on video you would normally expect to do most of your editing work "off line". In a later chapter we will be looking in detail at what video editing involves. At this stage I will just point out that you can either edit the original master tapes exposed in the camera by copying them on to another broadcast quality tape in an edit suite and working "on line". Alternatively you can copy your master tapes on to U-Matic or VHS or any suitable non broadcast format and edit them on much simpler equipment "off line". If you do that when your master tapes are copied before editing begins the time code recorded on your master will be duplicated on the copies. When off line editing is complete you simply log the time code references indicating where your cutting points are. The figures are then fed into computer controlled equipment in an on line edit suite which completes the editing process by matching the master tapes to the figures you provide.

On first acquaintance perhaps all this sounds very complicated. Don't worry! It is not a complex as it sounds, as you will find out if you read on. At this stage the important point is that if you work on line throughout you are going to end up with a much bigger editing bill than you will working off line at first and just going on line for the final processes. The broadcast quality equipment used for on line editing is very expensive. It costs a small fortune to equip an on line edit suite. To edit off line you only need one replay machine, one recorder and an edit controller. You can use low band U-Matic or even VHS and can hire equipment for a day for considerably less than you will have to pay for an hour in an on line suite. You can hire an off line cutting room by the day or the week. The equipment is reasonably portable and there are a number of companies which will deliver an off line suite to your home and allow you to hire it for as long as you wish. The cost of hiring that equipment should be built into your budget. The time needed for editing a video production will be about the same as it will is you shoot on film.

### 13. Travel and transport

This is another cost which needs to be accurately predicted if you are to avoid any nasty shocks. You must allow for the costs involved in getting yourself, your crew and any artistes to every location and back again. If you are shooting for long hours you may also need to allow for overnight accommodation. If more than half a dozen people are travelling to the same location from one area, it may be cheaper to hire a bus and take everyone out together. The same applies to air fares. If a number of people are travelling together approach all the airlines operating on that route and try to get the best deal. Travelling costs may not seem like a major item but when you add up how many journeys are involved the results may surprise you. If you are proposing to work alone or just with a friend and can go everywhere in your own car travel will not be a major item.

### 14. Insurance

At this stage of your career you may perhaps think that insurance is an instantly forgettable item. If that's your view I would urge you to think again. If you are hiring equipment your supplier will certainly charge you an insurance premium to cover the gear while it is in your hands and there other aspects of insurance which you ought to consider.

If you are proposing to shoot in any public place or involve anyone outside your immediate family, you should arrange some kind of public liability insurance cover. It is in your own interests to do so. If you are filming in a bar and, while you are supervising the rehearsal of a scene or watching a scene though a viewfinder, someone accidentally trips over one of the cables supplying your lights you could be in trouble. If the light crashes on someone you could find yourself facing a claim for damages and if you are not insured the outlook may be bleak. In my view it is essential to cover yourself and others against any accidents which may occur while your film or video is being made. Accidents can happen however well organised you are. In as long career in the industry I have seen a number of examples. I have watched lights crash down, narrowly missing people nearby, and one memorable afternoon filming in a foundry watched as a foundryman, who had been doing his job safely for many years, suddenly lost his grip on a crucible of moulten metal allowing it to crash to the ground inches away from where a camera crew was filming. It pays to be prepared and public liability insurance is an essential cost however small your production may be.

The insurance industry is, of course, greedy and welcomes every penny it can get so when you arrange your essential cover you may find they try to sell you other forms of cover. If you are shooting out of doors they may offer you a good weather cover. Policies differ from company to company but most will cover you against being unable to shoot due to rain or snow on a specified date. I personally have always found this kind of insurance is too expensive for the risks involved. If you are shooting on film you may be offered film stock and lab cover. Basically that involves covering your master film against any accidents which may befall it when it is being processed or printed and the cost of re-shooting any damaged scene(s). Again premiums tend to be high and I have never felt it was worth the sums involved but if you have a very elaborate scene which would be costly to shoot again it may be worth considering this kind of cover.

In over 30 years filming I have only once had to re-shoot due to a lab problem. Some rollers in a processing tank became jammed and put a very fine scratch on the edge of the negative of one roll. It was not a major fault. Most audiences probably would not have noticed it but we were shooting a professional production and when we saw the scratch on the screen as the rushes were projected we decided to re-shoot the scene the following day. It was an expensive operation because the scene involved four artistes in a hospital ward. We had taken over an empty hospital and furnished it to shoot that scene and all the furniture had been moved out at the end of the shoot. We had to put it all back and persuade the artistes to give an equally good performance for the re-shoot. It cost thousands of pounds but, if we had taken out lab insurance on all the productions we have done over the years, I think the total cost would have been much higher. You must assess the risks when you are preparing your budget make you own decisions

## 15. Profit and Overhead

The final costs you need to consider are the amount of profit you want to make and the overhead costs involved in making your production. For a showreel you may decide to ignore any profit and simply do all you can to ensure costs are minimised in the hope of eventually getting your money back. If you have persuaded a commercial sponsor to put up funds, you may wish to include a percentage of the budget as a profit. Later on, when you are involved in making professional productions for a living, calculating your level of profit will be extremely important, as we shall see later in the chapter dealing with running your own business.

Overhead costs are simply the costs you will incur in administration and the depreciation of any equipment you own. A professional production company will calculate the combined cost of office space, and any permanent administrative staff, heating, lighting, telephones, printing and stationary and various other costs and add a percentage of the annual cost to each production as an overhead. You should include a percentage of your total budget for contingencies to cover unexpected expenses you may find you have incurred. You can then add up the total figure and find out what making your showreel is likely to cost.

# CHAPTER 3
# DEVELOPING YOUR IDEAS

When you have decided what subject you are going to explore and whether you are going to make you programme on film or video you can begin to plan your production in detail. The principal aim of your showreel is for you to demonstrate your skills and as a result be able to persuade someone to give you a job but there are other aims you will also need to consider. Like all film and video producers you must satisfy the demands of the audiences who will see whatever you produce. If you are planning to produce a comedy that may mean entertaining them and making them laugh. If you are going to make a documentary it may mean encouraging them to learn something or increase their knowledge of the particular situation or subject you intend to deal with. If your production is sponsored your aim may be to promote a particular product or service or portray a particular image. There are many different possibilities and your aims, the requirements of any sponsor and the type of audience you expect to reach should all be considered before you start work.

## ATTEMPTING THE IMPOSSIBLE

It is always a mistake to try to do too much in one film or video. If you set out to promote a product it may not be practicable to teach people how to use it at the same time. Training and promotion are different aims and they often require different treatments. A colleague of mine recently produced a video about building site safety. It was sponsored by a construction company which had never sponsored a video before and produced with the advice and help of their safety experts. When the finished video was show to the company's senior management they were delighted. It got the necessary safety message across and showed the company in a very good light. The Managing Director was particularly pleased to see his company's name on the start of a thoroughly professional production and lost no time in expressing his delight.

"We ought to use it for sales promotion", he explained to my colleague who had to point out that, while the video made the sponsoring company look safe and efficient, it did not set out to sell the sort of services it wished to promote. It fulfilled the brief the sponsors had provided, which was to get across a number of safety points. To present an image of the company as a cost effective building contractor would require a different treatment. Additional shots would be required and the commentary would have to be re-written so it appealed to a different audience. The comments designed to interest safety officer would not interest an audiences of people considering placing building contracts. The aims of the video and the interests of the audience would not co-incide. And that is a pitfall you too must avoid. You must decide what you want to show and say and what audience you want your production to appeal to and settle for that.

So, what point or points do *you* want to make? What sort of audience will your production be shown to? Your choice of subject will probably help you to answer those questions. If a sponsor is involved his or her wishes may make the answer even more precise. For example, if you are making a video about a local charity you they will tell you what they want to show and why they want a video. They may wish to get a particular message across to people who are in a position to contribute to their funds. You will then know what you have to do and be able to work out the best way of achieving that objective and that is where your creative work will really begin.

## CHOOSING THE RIGHT TREATMENT

One of the nicest things about working in film and television is that it offers so many creative opportunities. You can make money and enjoy doing something creative at the same time, and that is a depressingly rare situation in industry today. Of course, not everyone exploits the creative possibilities to the full. Not every film or video is interesting to watch. We have all seen productions where we have prayed for the end titles to be reached as quickly as possible. It is so easy to make even an interesting subject boring to watch but with adequate research and a little imagination even the dullest subject can be brought to life.

You can look at any subject in a number of different ways.You have chosen the subject you want to film but how do you see that subject and how are you going to present it to an audience? As a producer you have complete freedom to influence your audience in any way you wish. You will first have to win their attention and then retain it as the programme progresses. You can do that by using a variety of production techniques which we will consider in detail as this book progresses. Your first task will be to decide how you are going to present your subject in terms of pictures and sounds and to outline those plans in a treatment and script.

## TREATMENTS AND SCRIPTS

What is the difference between a treatment and a script ? A treatment is really a synopsis explaining in plan language what you are going to show and how the subject will be presented. A script is written in two columns - on one side it lists the action you intend to show and on the other the dialogue, commentary or other sounds which will be heard at each point. Before you can prepare either of these documents you will need to carry out your research so you know all about the subject you intend to film. You will also need to decide whose eyes you use for the programme you intend to present. Let's consider a few examples.

## A SPONSOR'S BRIEF

For our first example let us assume that you have decided to try a suggestion I made earlier and approach a local charity for sponsorship. You have managed to persuade the owners of an old peoples home to contribute to your costs if you make a video about their activities. You have carried out some research and now know that the home has 50 permanent residents. The oldest has just celebrated her hundred and first birthday. The home is entirely supported by voluntary contributions from the public and by a collection taken at a Christmas carol concert held each year in the local church. The management want to extend the home and are trying to raise funds to build more rooms. Your video will be used to encourage people to contribute to a building appeal fund. That is all you have so far discovered. You have managed to persuade the management of the home to give you some money and now the success of the video is up to you.

## WHOSE POINT OF VIEW ?

Now you have got your subject and enough money to help you to explore it on video but how are you going to do it ? You know what the management of the home want to show. They want more people to see how they look after their elderly residents in the hope that it will encourage audiences to part with money which will enable them to care for even more. How are you going to get the message across on video ? There are plenty of possibilities. You could do it the boring way, starting with the Chairman of the Management

Board talking to camera. He would no doubt be delighted to "say a few words" and you could then cut away from him to show the activities he describes. The Chairman would be delighted but others might not share his enthusiasm. It would be better to choose a treatment which is more original. How else could you do it ? Why not put this book down for a few minutes and try and think up you own ideas based on the information provided above and then read on.

I wonder what ideas you have had. Here are some you may have considered. You could start with the annual carol concert and watch people arriving and taking part. It should be quite joyful occasion with plenty of colour and life. You could end your opening sequence with a shot of one of the elderly residents in church and then mix through to see where she normally lives. A few sentences of voice over commentary could set the scene and get you audience interested in the subject. You might perhaps say something along the following lines :

" For Dorothy this is the highlight of the year. At the age of 86 she doesn't get out much but once a year she makes a determined effort to thank God for the benefits she enjoys in the rest of the year. A collection taken during the service helps to provide those benefits and keep Dorothy and her friends in safety and comfort". In 30 seconds, using a treatment like that you have introduced your subject and a character who you could then use to link later sequences together and you have avoided the boredom of a "talking head" by not featuring the Chairman.

## AN ALTERNATIVE OPENING

Another way of starting a video on the same subject would be to start with shots of the home's oldest resident. She is surrounded by friends and about to blow out the candles on a birthday cake. Again you could use a few sentences of voice over commentary to set the scene :

"For Mary this is a special birthday. She is a hundred and one today and at that age blowing out candles can be quite an effort".

You could then cut to old photographs of her family on a table nearby and explain that when her husband died 25 years ago Mary found herself alone for the first time in her life. Arthritis and failing sight soon confined her to a chair and life began to lose its attractions then, she heard of the Eventide Home and for the first time met the friends who are celebrating with her today. At this point your commentary could end and the camera could show her friends gathering round the cake to sing "happy birthday". Opening titles could then be superimposed.

## WINNING AUDIENCE INTEREST

I have suggested two ways of starting a video. They are not very good ideas. You have probably thought of much better ones but the suggestions I have made show how you can use pictures and sound to introduce a subject in a very short time. It is important to win the interest of your audiences from the outset. When your video is shown they will be chatting and doing other things before it begins and you must immediately grab their attention and make them feel that this is a programme they really need to watch. You can do that in many different ways. I have suggested two already. Now let's consider a third. In stead of starting with the main subject ( life in the old people's home), you could perhaps start with shots of young people practising karate. You might show someone breaking bricks with his head ( yes, they really do that!) and then show some one else smashing a plank with an open hand. A commentary could again set the scene :

" There are some whose strength seems almost unlimited but for Mary, turning a page in a book requires just as much effort". You could then dissolve from a shot of a young karate expert to show an old lady whose hands have been withered away by arthritis. She is trying to hold a book and turn a page. With her mis-shapen hands the page proves impossible to grip. From that point on you could explain how, when this sort of damage occurs, it is difficult to lead a normal life without help. Fortunately for Mary she has found it. The video could then go on to see the activities which take place in the home during a week, seen through Mary's eyes.

You may think all those ideas are awful and have much better ones yourself but they will at least encourage you to think and realise that there are many way of dealing with every subject. Your showreel is the same. You can take a boring unimaginative approach or try to make your subject interesting to watch and to listen to. Never forget your audience. As you make your plans ask yourself how they are likely to react. Have you made what you want to show and say easy to follow or have you left something unexplained? Are you using your soundtrack to make additional points or are you simply describing what they can see for themselves? You will find there is a lot of satisfaction in working out ideas.

## PLANNING YOUR SOUNDTRACK

When you are considering what kind of treatment to give your film or video don't forget your soundtrack. Films and videos are made up of pictures and sounds and they should both be used as creatively as possible. Many video producers tend to under estimate the importance of sound and that is a mistake you should try to avoid. Your soundtrack can include music, sound effects, a commentary or synchronised sound interviews all of which can help to bring your showreel to life. You have probably seen films and videos made by people who have not bothered much about sound. There is a commentary but no sound effects and consequently the scenes do not come to life. Sound effects can act as a punctuation mark, allowing the mind to re-focus after sentences of dialogue. They can add atmosphere and make pictures more interesting to watch.

**SYNCHRONSIED AND WILD DIALOGUE**

Dialogue can be used in various ways. It can be *synchronised* or used *wild*. Synchronised dialogue is spoken in view of the camera. You can see who is speaking and his or her lip movements match the words you are hearing on the soundtrack, as in any interview conducted "in vision". Wild sound is spoken by people out of vision. Voice over commentaries are often recorded wild - i.e. without any picture. They are then edited to fit the pictures in the cutting room in a process known as "laying" commentary or overlaying sound. You can use interviews creatively too. You can shoot an interview in vision but you do not have to see it all when you make your edited version. You can start or end with the interviewee in vision and cut away to show what he or she is describing, overlaying the sound. For example, imagine you have filmed an interview with the owner of a new theme park. In the interview he has described some of the attractions the new park has to offer. When you start editing you can begin with a shot of the owner in vision and superimpose his name and position so the audience knows whose voice they are hearing. After a sentence or two you can keep his voice going on the soundtrack and cut away to show the attractions he describes. Using shots and sound like that will make your video more interesting to watch and, when you are planning the treatment you intend to use, you should give an equal amount of thought to your pictures and soundtrack.

## WORKING WITHOUT A COMMENTARY

We have so far considered one possible subject (life in that old people's home) and looked at a number of ways of exploring it on film or video. The ideas we considered all involved a fairly straightforward documentary treatment with a voice over commentary. That commentary could be intercut with comments made by the home's residents speaking either in vision or wild. It is equally easy to make a programme without any commentary at all or with a minimal amount simply being used to link sequences together. You can use synchronised sound throughout, intercutting interviews or using comments made by the participants either in vision or wild. You can just settle for music and sound effects and try to make the pictures tell their own story. All these possibilities should be considered when you plan your treatment. Let's look at another example.

## BRINGING ARGUMENTS TO LIFE

Let us assume that on this occasion it's a local newspaper story which has given you an idea for your showreel. There is a report in it this week that a property developer is planning to buy your local cinema. He is not interested in films and wants to pull it down and build a supermarket. The idea has aroused a lot of controversy. The paper reports the views of local people who feel it is disgraceful and should not be allowed. Conservationists point out that the cinema is a beautiful building which contains many fine features. An old projectionist who has worked there since he left school is heartbroken at the proposals. The newspaper report introduces you to a subject which you feel could make an interesting video and you decide to explore the possibilities in depth.

Your research reveals that the developer who want to build the supermarket is a very wealthy man who has interests in a number of businesses. He has been involved in controversial schemes before and a few months ago was taken to court for failing to meet the obligations of a contract. He says he wants to improve facilities in the area and feels his new supermarket will be welcomed by shoppers. Others suspect he is only interested in making a profit.

## TELLING A STORY IN PICTURES AND SOUNDS

How are you going to explore the subject of that newspaper article on film or video? You may perhaps decide that you want to film inside and outside the cinema to show its character and beauty. You want to interview cinemagoers and the old projectionist who has worked there all his life. People living nearby will be asked for their views and you will try to get an interview with the developer and show architects at work on his plans. When you have obtained all those different views you will put the programme together in the cutting room. You have immense power in your hands. You can put that video together in a way which make the developer sound like a progressive industrialist with great ideas from which everyone will benefit. You can also make him seem like a money grabbing shark who is determined to destroy a building no one can replace, or you can present both arguments with equal emphasis and let your audiences decide. It's up to you.

## PLANNING INTERVIEWS

To get whatever point of view you wish to put across to your audience you will need suitable pictures and sounds to work with and that is where preparing a treatment and script will prove invaluable. You will not be able to script your interviews, but you can script the questions you intend to ask to get the sort of answers you want to hear. If you ask the wrong questions or put them the wrong way you may get one word answers which you will be unable to use. For example, if you ask people living near the cinema is they think the proposed new development is a good idea or not, they will probably answer "yes" or "no". That will not help you but if you try to discover their views in a slightly different way they will probably produce longer answers and reveal their feelings. You could try asking them," How do you think the proposed supermarket will affect this area"? When it comes to the cinema you could ask if they have ever been inside it and if they have, what they felt about what they saw and about the future it may face. You should expect to shoot a lot of material. That is quite normal when interviewing the public, but if you ask the right questions and shoot the right shots you will be able to put together a very powerful video. It's a different technique to the one we discussed earlier. You will be using interviews and voice over comments from the people who are involved, to tell a story they all feel strongly about and that is another technique you could use for your showreel.

## MAINTAINING A COMMERCIAL SENSE

I hope by now you are beginning to see how much power you as a film or video maker can enjoy when you have mastered the various skills involved. The world is full of interesting subjects. Unfortunately, in a world which is motivated primarily by money, many of the most interesting subject are not particularly commercial. I have had to abandon many subjects I have wanted to film because I did not feel they would interest a commercial sponsor or be of wide enough interest to recover their production cost from subsequent television showings or the sale of videos. If you are to make money you will need to do the same. You will have to prevent yourself being tempted to shoot subjects you feel are tremendous but which no one else will back. Your showreel will principally show the results of your talent but, if it is to be a success, the subject it explores must interest the people who will see it. If you want to get your money back you will be well advised to pick a subject which has good commercial prospects. Remember making films and videos is principally a business and, while it can be enormously enjoyable, it's making enough money to live on which will probably need to be your principal objective.

## TESTING YOUR CREATIVITY

To encourage you to test your creative abilities and use your imagination I am going to outline two more possible subjects for a film or video and invite you to consider how you would present them to an audience. I will then tell you what others have done with the same subjects and you can assess their efforts against yours. We will consider a school film and a holiday video.

## MAKING A SCHOOL VIDEO

When you were at school you may have been involved in making either a school film or a video. Many people who eventually build careers for themselves in the industry start in that way. Now I am gong to ask you to take that work a stage further. You are now a professional producer and know a bit more about making films and videos. You have been asked to make a school video to show parents what your school is all about. How are you going to deal with the subject? Again you may care to put this book down and work out your own ideas. We will then see how others have dealt with the same challenge.

Your ideas may well be better than the ones I can now report. In any event I am sure you  enjoyed working them out.  It is quite a challenge to take a subject as broad as life in a school and try to find a suitable storyline for a film or video.  I have seen many different treatments.  One started with a new boy arriving at the beginning of term. He was clearly very nervous and the opening shots were taken from his head height making the older boys and masters seem like giants.  It was an effective opening and the video then went on to observe the activities of that school through the newcomer's eyes.  It worked well and in 20 minutes we got a good idea of what went on and we began to get to know and like the boy as he gradually got involved in a new way of life.

Another school video I saw recently explored life at a leading English public school.  It started with shots of the Headmaster addressing a meeting of parents. They were sitting in chair on a lawn in the shadow of an old abbey church.  The Headmaster told a short and funny story - something about cannibals eating a missionary and saying he gave them their first real taste of Christianity. The camera then pulled back across the lawns to give a general view of all the school buildings. As the view widened to show a magnificent setting we heard a few lines of commentary:

" A summer day on an English lawn and an opportunity for the Headmaster to recall past achievements and outline future plans. It's a pleasant occasion but what happens when the parents have left ?  What is life normally like here, in an English public school"?

The main titles were superimposed at that point and the video then explored everyday life in the school. There was no more commentary until the end of the programme.

Just music, sound effects the comments of boys and masters, carefully edited to provide a soundtrack. It was fascinating to watch. The treatment was simple and effective and the video was well received all over the world because it was so visual and appealing.

## ORIGINAL TREATMENTS FOR WELL EXPLORED SUBJECTS

There are many ways of dealing with every subject. How did you decide to present your school film ? And how would you handle a holiday video? Holiday promotional programmes are among the hardest to make. There are so many examples of bad practice. We have all seen programmes which extol the virtues of the places being shown so much that by the end you never want to see or hear of them again. It is difficult to be original but it can be done. Here's an example.

The Tourist Board of a very well known island approached a video company to ask them to make a promotional video. The island had many attractions but, like so many tourist destinations, when you added them up most of them could also be found in a many other places. What was needed was an original idea and the producers found it. They did not want to use a conventional treatment with a formal narrator reading a commentary written like a brochure. They felt the secret of success lay in who appeared to be telling the story they had to tell. They had to get a lot of facts across but their did not want to do it in the usual way. They considered many alternatives. They could follow a famous personality round the island, but that idea had been used many times before. They wanted to find a treatment which was different and they succeeded.

## A DIFFERENT APPROACH

Their video started at a different destination. The opening scene showed a man with his wife and family trying to control a boat which they had hired. It was a funny scene which quickly showed that the husband was a know-all who never listened to anyone. In 30 seconds audiences got the picture and, as we saw the boat put out to sea, we heard the husband assure his wife that she had nothing to worry about. He knew what he was doing and all would be well.

In the next scene we saw the same boat and family some hours later. It was very quiet and the boat was hardly moving. It was marooned in fog. It soon became clear that the know-all husband did not know how to use the radar and had no idea where the boat was. He climbed on deck to find out if he could see anything and spied a stretch of land ahead. He shouted to see if anyone could hear him and a muffled voice replied. Full of new confidence dad returned to the wheelhouse and set course for the misty shore.

" There you are", he told his wife. "I told you I knew where we were. If only you would listen". The boat reached the shore and for the first time we saw the owner of the voice we had heard. He looked happy and fit and shouted a welcome. The know-all replied in French believing he had successfully brought his family to the French port he had been aiming for when they had set out, but the man on the shore spoke English. It soon became clear that the boat had landed twenty miles short of it's intended destination, on an island the family had never intended to visit.

## USING A PERSONAL VIEW FOR NARRATION

The islander, whose voice had greeted them, explained where they were and added re-assuringly.

"Don't worry about the mist. It's early yet. In an hour it will be transformed". As he spoke the sun came out ( thanks to a dissolve to scenes shot later !) and we saw the island as the Tourist Board wanted it to be seen - an idyllic place which anyone would be delighted to visit. As the video progressed the islander's voice acted as a voice over commentary telling us about the attractions of the island he knew and obviously loved. That enabled it to be written much less formally than it would have been if it had been read by a newsreader type of voice. In stead is saying "they" he was able to say "we" or "you" and as a result the whole video had a much more human touch. It was an original approach with an opening which worked well on the screen, though it is quite difficult to describe in words, and it was another way of bringing originality to a well explored subject. When the video was produced the islander and the other characters involved were all played by actors and the programme was a great success.

## ALTERNATIVE WAYS OF DEALING WITH THE SAME SUBJECT

I have since seen two other videos on the same subject. One saw the island thorough the eyes of a newspaperman who had been sent to cover an international conference. He soon got bored with the conference and decided to see what the island was like. His adventures provided a framework for the story. The third video on the same subject started with a carnival and then went on to look at the island's everyday life. It let the camera do the exploring with a minimum of commentary. All three videos worked by presenting the attractions they had to portray in very different ways and you will find you can present the subject you have chosen to deal with in your showreel in a similar manner. You can use voice over narration or build your sound-track up with interviews or random comments from those seen in the action. You can use those comments "in sync" with the picture or "wild". You can make the audience see your programme through many different eyes. When you work out your treatment you will be able to pick the one which appeals to you most.

## FROM TREATMENT TO SCRIPT

When you have completed a treatment which explains what you are going to show and say and how you are going to do it, you can start to prepare a script. As I explained before, scripts are written in two columns. On the left hand side you list the action and on the right, any dialogue or other sound. When you write the action column you will need to precisely describe what you want to show and how you want it to be shown and to do that you will need to understand basic film and video grammar.

## CHOOSING THE RIGHT VIEWPOINT

Every scene can be observed from a number of different points and when you are writing your script you will need to specify how you want each shot to be filmed. You can choose any of six different viewpoints -

1. *Distant shot.* (Abbreviated DS). This is sometimes referred to as a very long shot (VLS.) A general view covering a wide area.

2. *Long shot.* (LS) A general view of a location or subject but not as wide as a distant shot. A LS might show a complete house while a DS would show the house and its surroundings When filming people a LS would normally show the whole person or a group of people.

3. *Medium Shot* (MS) Also known as a mid shot. A shot taken at normal viewing distance cutting at the waistline

4. *Close medium shot* (CMS). Head and shoulders

5. *Close up* (CU) A shot taken close enough to reveal detail. For example a face or hands.

6.*Big close up.*(BCU) A every close view - for example a person's eyes.

In an ideal situation, when you write your script you will be able to specify how you want to shoot every single shot. In practice you will find you cannot always do that. If you are making a documentary like the ones I have mentioned earlier, you may simply have to plan an overall framework and will not be able to script individual shots. You will end up with a list of the subjects you want to cover and have to choose the right angles to film then from when you are shooting. If you are writing a dramatised story you may be able to pre-plan every shot and angle and list exactly what you want to show in detail on your script.

Even if it is impractical to prepare a detailed shooting script giving full details of action and sound you should still do as much preparation as you can before you shoot anything. Take that travel programme for example. It was not possible to produce a shooting script for the whole video in advance because the producers could not be sure what would be going at all the attractions they had to include when they were available to film, but they did script the opening scene in detail and make a list of everything else they needed include. If they had not done that, they could have ended up in the cutting room with some vital aspect of the subject missing. So, give yourself a plan and, if possible write a script. Here is the opening scene from a safety training video to give you an idea of what a documentary shooting script looks like.

*1. Ext day. LS. Library
shot. Jet aircraft flying
in close formation across
an airfield.CAMERA CONCENTRATES
on two aircraft flying very
close together. Their wing tips
touch and they crash to the
ground.*

*Sound effects.*

CUT

*2.DS. Spectators at airfield.
As planes crash they run
in all directions. The planes
catch fire,*

*Sound effects.
Crash/Screams*

CUT

*3. LS. A lorry parked nearby
bursts into flames*

*NARRATOR:
When the
unexpected
happened on a
summer afternoon,
fifty people died as
a result of an
accident no one
could ever have
predicted.*

CUT

*4. MS.Families run for cover*
*as flames engulf their cars*

*NARRATOR :*
*It was a tragedy*
*but every year*
*hundreds die and*
*thousands more are*
*seriously injured in*
*accidents which*
*could nearly*
*always be foreseen.*

*DISSOLVE*

*5.Int factory.Day.*
*LS. Fork lift truck being driven*
*round a corner.It is*          *Sound fx.*
*overloaded with three*
*large boxes of metal parts.*

*6.CMS. The truck driver's*
*view of the way ahead. It*
*is obscured because he*
*is carrying too many boxes.*
*He can't see where he is*
*going.*

*7.LS. The truck and load*
*approaching camera.*
*CAMERA TRACKS BACK. We see*
*there is a man mending a*
*hole in the floor. He is*
*directly in the truck's path.*

*8. CMS. The Truck, driving
from R to L at speed.*

*9. CU. Man mending floor.
He suddenly hears the truck
and turns to look L to R.
He realizes it is going to hit
him. CAMERA CONCENTRATES ON
his face.*

*10. CMS. The truck approaching.
FAST ZOOM INTO BCU of metal
in the boxes. CAMERA TILTS
wildly up to ceiling as
if it had been hit by the truck.*          *Fx: Crash*

*DISSOLVE TO*

*11. MS. Man who was mending the floor
buried under overturned truck and
crushed boxes. A spinning wheel is
the only sign of life.
SUPERIMPOSE TITLE :
The Common Sense Guide to Safety At Work*

That is the first page of a shooting script for a very successful documentary. In addition to specifying the camera's viewpoint for each shot you will have noticed that it provided a number of other directions telling the production team what needed to be filmed and recorded at every stage. It showed how the editor will move from shot to shot. In most instances it called for an instant transition by making a cut but between scenes four and five the transition was gradual. The script explained that the shot of people fleeing from burning cars should gradually disappear and be replaced by a shot of the fork truck approaching - a transition known as a dissolve or a mix. You will also have noticed that the commentary was economical. There were just enough words to set the scene and link the first two sequences together. Like all good commentaries, it added something to the action. It did not describe exactly what the audience could see for themselves. It provided them with additional facts, as a commentary should.

Now perhaps you feel you are ready to write your own script or at least prepare a detailed outline of what you intend to say and show. When you have done that, you should visit all the locations at which you intend to shoot and make sure they are suitable for what the shots you have in mind.

## LOCATION "RECCYS".

The dictionary definition of reconnoitre explains that it means "to approach and try to learn the position of strategic features". In the film world the word is usually abbreviated to "reccy". When you go to inspect a location and see if it is going to be suitable for filming the scenes you have in mind what features should you look for ? The first thing to check is the power supply. Are there enough electric sockets or will you need to run extension leads from somewhere else? If you are proposing to use a lot of lights you may need an electrician to connect a special supply rather than use ordinary plugs and sockets. What is the normal lighting like? It is predominantly daylight or is there more tungsten lighting? Are you going to have the place to yourself or are other people going to be around?

When seeking permission to film you will often find that people who know nothing about filming will agree to let you in without really appreciating what is involved. They assume you will just arrive with a small camera and take a few simple shots. If you subsequently turn up with lights, reflectors, cables and a full a production team they may not be so happy and, if they change their minds at that stage, you could really be in trouble. So it is always worth making sure the owner or whoever is in charge of all the locations at which you are seeking permission to film, fully understands what is going to happen. Explain exactly what you want to do and what that will involve and then put it in writing so there can be no doubts in anyones mind.If you are filming in areas which are used by the public it is particularly important to make sure they will not be in your way or you in theirs.

## FILMING IN PUBLIC PLACES

If you are going to shoot in a street or some other place open to the public you may need police permission or a permit of some kind. The world is full of petty officials who thoroughly enjoy wielding a little bit of power and if you need a particular form and do not have it they will pounce and delay your filming. A few weeks ago we were shooting a girl feeding pigeons in a park. Just when she was surrounded by the birds we had waited ages to see, an official arrived and asked if we had a permit to film. We were unaware that one was required and were not causing any disturbance but the little man was determined to have his way and exercise the only authority he has probably ever had and we were unable to continue. So, if you are going to shoot in any public place,it is worth asking in advance if you are going to need any official approvals

## A SOUND RECCY

If you are planning to record location sound when you shoot, your reccy should include an assessment of the overall noise levels and the acoustics of each location. Are there any background sounds like air conditioning units or unwanted noises from nearby building sites? We recently had to shoot some scenes in a hotel. It looked beautiful in the brochure and the manager assured us we would be able to work without interruption is the conference suite. It all sounded perfect but as usual we decided to check it out. When we called a week before filming was due to start we found the hotel was half a mile from a busy airport. With planes taking off and landing every thirty seconds, it was obviously unsuitable for shooting dialogue scenes and another location had to be found.

## ANYTHING TO PAY ?

You should also check if you are going to have to pay for the use of your locations. You will probably find that some places will be happy to let you in without a charge if you do not cause any problems and leave everything as you found it when you depart. If you are going to use power for lighting or need to use a telephone you should make an agreed contribution to the costs involved. In other places you will find they want a fee to let you past the front door. All these points should be established well in advance of any filming date to avoid confusion or embarrassment later.

## PREPARING A SHOOTING SCHEDULE

When you have a script or a detailed shooting plan and have found suitable locations you can prepare the last documents you need to produce before you start to film - a call sheet and shooting schedule. You will probably not be shooting your film or video in the order in which the scenes will eventually be seen in the final edited version. For example, scene 1 and scene 26 may need to be shot at the same location and the shots which will eventually be seen between them and  need to be shot elsewhere. As it obviously makes sense to shoot all the scenes you need at each location in one visit you will inevitably find you are shooting many shots out of script order. To ensure shots are not accidentally missed out and to make certain that everyone and everything you need is in the right place at the right time, you should prepare a detailed breakdown of your script in filming order.

Your schedule should list the scenes you are proposing to shoot on each date. State the day and date and give the location address or addresses and telephone number(s). Indicate the time at which you intend to start. Underneath those headings you should indicate which scenes you intend to shoot and the order in which you are planning to shoot them in. If artistes are involved they will need to know which lines they need to be word perfect on first and will not thank you if you tell them you are going to start with scene nine and then decide at the last minute to shoot scene thirteen. Your schedule should also list any vital props.

## TOO MUCH PAPERWORK ?

You may perhaps wonder if it is really necessary to prepare all this paperwork when you know perfectly well in your own mind what is going to happen. You have told everyone else involved what they must do, and perhaps feel that enough preparatory work has already been done. If that is your view, I would urge you to think again because if you do not change your mind you are quite likely to arrive at one of your locations and find you have forgotten to bring some vital prop or someone who is crucial to the scene has gone to the wrong address. Such problems can always be solved but correcting them takes time and it will delay your shooting. If everything is planned on paper and the schedule is checked before you set off each day, the chances of making an error will be minimised.

Arrangements with artistes should always be confirmed in writing and agents will often want a contract to be signed before shooting begins. In any event you should write stipulating the part each artiste is being asked to play and listing the filming dates and the times agreed. State what fee you have offered and what that covers. If you do not put your deals in writing you will run the risk of having someone come back to you at a later date and claiming he or she is owed more than you agreed. Make the facts clear and everyone will benefit.

## A REALISTIC SCHEDULE

When you prepare your shooting schedule don't try to cram in too much work each day. Remember not every scene will work out as you envisage first time. You are bound to encounter unexpected problems and delays, as we will see in the next chapter. So, allow time to get to each location and unpack the equipment and set it up. Leave more time for rehearsals and for several takes and then you will not find you are rushing to beat the clock at the end of the day. If your schedule includes any overseas shooting, it is worth remembering that after a long flight no one will feel like stepping off the plane and immediately starting work. I had to shoot some scenes in Australia recently. I flew out from London and after 23 hours in an aircraft sitting next to a lady who seemed to be able to talk without drawing breath for most of the time, I did not feel like doing anything except possibly committing suicide when I arrived. Fortunately the schedule had allowed for a rest day on arrival.

## INTERNATIONAL SHOOTING

When you are flying from place to place you will probably have to meet excess baggage payments for transporting your equipment. Always check in  for your flight at least an hour earlier than you would check in without the gear in case you have problems with customs or with the airline. Most airlines are very security conscious and they will want to check any electrical equipment you have before you can board. In some countries you will need to list your equipment on a special customs carnet. That is a form which is internationally accepted as a declaration of goods. As you pass from country to country, customs officers at each point of arrival and departure will keep a copy of the form. You must ensure they sign or stamp the appropriate copies when you arrive and leave each country. If you move on without the appropriate official stamp you may find you have to pay an import or an export tax at your next destination or when you get back.

## SUMMARY

Let's summarise. When you first decide to make your film or video you may believe that all you have to do is think of a good subject and go out and film. In practice there is usually a lot more to it than that.You will find your showreel is easier to make, and the end result will probably be better, if you meticulously plan every stage of production. First find a good subject. Research it and think about how you are going to explore it on film or video. Decide whose eyes you are going to see your subject through and how you are going to present it to your audience. Think carefully about that audience. What are they going to appreciate most and how can you make your film or video appeal to them ?

When you have worked out every shot and every viewpoint, find suitable locations and contact the other people you want to help you turn your ideas into a professional video or film. Visit each location and look out for anything which might make it difficult to shoot. Negotiate fees for artistes and locations and put the deals you have agreed in writing. Make a list of any special props you require and then prepare a shooting schedule specifying what scenes you will shoot on each day. Show where they will be filmed and who needs to be there on that occasion. List the props you are going to need in each place and carry out a final check before you set off to film. If you are shooting with equipment you are not familiar with, it is probably worth taking the camera out before you film anything important and shooting a test. It is much better to get used to unfamiliar gear when you are not in a rush or faced with a busy shooting schedule.

**SHOOTING A TEST**

It is very easy to make mistakes without being immediately aware of the consequences. Shooting on video for example, if the back focus on your camera is not correctly aligned or the view-finder focus does not match your eyes, your shots may be soft. The problem may be almost imperceptible in a view-finder but when your tapes are shown on a larger monitor it may be embarrassingly clear. If you are shooting on film and are using a film stock you are not used to working with, you may get the exposure wrong or not be sure how much latitude you have to work with. Shooting a test before you do anything important will help you avoid unnecessary disasters.

When all your preparations have been completed you can start shooting and in the next chapter we will see what you may encounter.

# CHAPTER 4
# IN PRODUCTION

Now you are ready to shoot. After checking your schedule you can set off for your first location. In this chapter we are going consider the main things you will need to know about when you are shooting indoors and at outside locations. We will look at each situation from two points of view. We will see what you need to do if you are working on film and then consider the same situation on video. I do not intend to go into too much technical detail. My purpose is to give you enough knowledge to be able to go out and get started. When you put the basic guide-lines I shall outline into practice, you will learn a lot more and that is what making movies is all about. There is always something to learn. So, let's move off to the first location and see what you are like to encounter.

## ESTABLISHING A BASE

When you arrive the first thing to do is to get yourself a base. Keep all the gear together, preferably in an area where you can plug in a battery charger and set up any video play-back equipment. It should be a place which can properly secured. Unfortunately not everyone is honest and if equipment is left unattended it may be stolen. It is a mistake to assume that everyone is a good guy where you are working, as I discovered when we were filming in a cathedral and had a box of filters stolen !

When you have checked to see that all the gear you need has arrived at the location you can start to prepare the camera and lights for the first scene. Let us assume you are making a video about that old peoples home we talked about earlier. Your opening shot is going to show the lady who is 101 blowing out the candles on her birthday cake. She is sitting in a chair by a window with the cake on a low table in front of her. There are several friends standing alongside. You want to set up your camera facing the old lady in a position which will enable you to get a close up of the cake and some cutaway shots of her friends from the same angle without moving the tripod. The room is not very light. The window lets in some light but it is not a bright day and the only other light is coming from a standard lamp which is beside the table. You are going to have to provide more light to get a suitable exposure, so let's see what you must you do.

## CHOOSING THE RIGHT LIGHTS

Your equipment includes a portable lighting kit which consists of four redhead 650w lamps with stands and accessories and you are going to need to use them for this opening scene. When you have assembled the lamp heads on their stands you can decide where you want to place each lamp and what accessories you need to use. Two factors will influence your decisions - the colour temperature of the available light in the room you are using and the effect you want to convey.

## USING LIGHTS CREATIVELY

A good lighting cameraman can make a scene look bright and cheerful or gloomy and depressing by using lights in various ways. With a small portable lighting kit you cannot be immensely creative but you can still do quite a lot. You may care to try conducting an experiment. Get a friend to sit in a chair and assemble two lights. Place one on the left hand side of your subject and position it about three metres away. You can then put the other light in front and to the right of your model. Now if you put the left light on flood and the right light on spot you will give the model's figure and face more shape than if you have both lights at the same intensity and the same distance from your subject. Try moving the lights round to different positions and varying their intensity by switching from spot to flood. On most modern portable lamps you can make that adjustment by just turning the base of the lamp holder. Turn it to the right and the lamp will become a spot. Turn it the other way and it will become softer as it moves into the flood position. By conducting a simple experiment like this you will discover how much can be achieved by using even the simplest lighting. You can make someone look menacing by lighting them dramatically from a low angle. You can cast a hard shadow and a dim background and create a bit of drama or you can softly illuminate the whole area and make it seem welcoming and friendly.

## LIGHTING ACCESSORIES

You can control the output of your lights in several different ways. I have already described the focusing controls which will enable you to move from flood to spot. You will also find that most modern lamps are supplied with hinged metal doors. They are known as *barn doors* and they can be opened or closed to control the shape of the beam and to eliminate any unwanted spill of light. You an also soften the glare from your lights by hanging spun glass fibre sheets in front of them. You can buy or hire fitted diffusing filters but most people use sheets of *"spun"* which they cut to a size which enables them to be attached to barn doors with clothes pegs or other suitable clips. If you are shooting on video you will often find a soft light with a lower contrast ratio produces better results than a hard direct light.

## INDIRECT LIGHTING

You do not have to point lights directly at the subjects you are going to shoot. If you want a more gentle effect you can bounce light off reflectors, walls or ceilings which are themselves out of shot. If you do that you will of course lose quite a lot  light but you will also lose any strong shadows. If you are going to bounce light off walls or ceilings make sure the areas you are using are white because if they are coloured you will simply reflect the hue they are coloured in.

## ASSESSING COLOUR TEMPERATURES

The colour temperature of each scene needs to be considered before you can shoot. As you may already know, colour temperature is measured on a scale known as the Kelvin scale. If you want a really detailed explanation of all the principles of colour photography you should read the Focal Encyclopedia of Film and Television Techniques (Focal Press), which gives a far more detailed analysis of this specialized subject than I intend to provide here. The key point you need to bear in mind when you are actually filming is that there are two main types of light - artificial (usually tungsten) light and daylight.  The colour temperature of daylight is normally around 6,500 degrees K.   Tungsten lights are normally around 3,200 degrees K but not all artificial lights are the same. Fluorescent lights are not the same colour temperature as tungsten bulbs and if you film in fluorescent light and do not check the colour balance you may find your pictures have an overall cast which is slightly blue or green. The key thing to avoid is mixing light sources of different colour temperatures. To see what that can mean in practice let's go back to our old lady sitting in the window and see what the shot means from a cameraman's point of view in terms of colour temperature and lighting.

## PROBLEMS WITH MIXED LIGHT

Through the window we can see daylight (6500 degrees K). The lady sitting in front of the window is silhouetted by it. It makes the side of her face which nearest the camera look very dark indeed and that would not look good on film or video so, before you can shoot you will need to fill in the shadowy areas by using some artificial lighting. If you set up one tungsten redhead light and put it on full flood, you will be able to fill in most of the shadows and reduce the overall contrast. If you use two lights and place them different distances away from the subject with one on the left and one on the right, you can make the shape of the lady's face more interesting. Now you have enough light to give you a reasonable exposure but you still have a colour temperature problem. Your tungsten lights are giving you light of one colour temperature (3200K) and the daylight coming through the window is giving you another (6500K). If you shoot on film using stock intended for tungsten light or if you use a tungsten colour filter setting on a video camera, the subjects in the foreground will look alright but the view outside the window will go blue. If you use a daylight film or a the 6500 filter on your video camera the view through the window will be fine but the people in the foreground will look far too orange. So how can you solve this dilemma ?

## BALANCING DAYLIGHT

The easiest way of dealing with the problem we have just considered is to balance the artificial lights to match the colour temperature of the daylight by placing dichroic blue filters over each lamp either in front of or behind the sheets of "spun". Dichroic filters cut out certain wavelengths of light and effectively convert the colour temperature of your lights from 3200K to 6500K. They also reduce their intensity by quite a considerable amount. You can hire glass dichroics with your lighting kit or cut sheets of dichroic filter material and suspend them in front of the lights using the same pegs or clips you use for glass fibre spun.

## CAMERA FILTERS

You have now fixed filters to your lights and made them the same colour temperature as the daylight coming though the window. All you have to do now is to ensure your camera and the tape or film you are using is suitable for the type of light you are now using. If you are shooting on film, you may be filming on stock balanced for tungsten light shooting or on daylight stock. You can use tungsten stock when you are filming in daylight if you put a Wratten 85 filter over the camera lens. If you are shooting the scene we have just considered and have placed dichroic filters in front of your lights to balance them to the daylight coming through the window, you can expose on normal daylight stock.

If you are shooting on video you will find colour temperature filters are built into the camera. You just have to choose the right one. Turn the filter select button, which you will normally find alongside the lens, and then look through the view-finder. You will find it will tell you which filter you have chosen. The indicator will not usually stay on all the time. It will simply flash on for a few seconds as you move each filter into place, so choose the one you require and check your selection. You should choose 6500K for the daylight balanced scene we have just discussed.

## USING A WHITE BALANCE

If you are shooting on video you will find your camera has a control labelled "white balance". It is provided to give you complete control of the colour temperature of every scene you shoot. To use it effectively, first do everything you can to make sure the colour temperature of all your light sources is the same in the way we have discussed. You can then select the correct camera filter. Next get a large piece of white card or a sheet of white paper and point the lens at it or at anything else which is completely white and in the area you have lit. Press the white balance switch and the camera will automatically adjust its colour balance to give a pure white. You can the go ahead and shoot your scene. If your lights are all correctly balanced the adjustment will just be a formality but if there are some fluorescent lights as well as the tungsten ones you have provided they may give a slight colour cast which white balancing can eliminate.

**CORRECTING COLOURS AFTER SHOOTING**

It is important to try to get a reasonably accurate colour balance when you are shooting but if you forget to do it, there are still steps you can take to correct colour values later in production. On video, when you are editing you can correct the colour balance scene by scene electronically and on film rushes and show prints can be colour graded before they are printed. At that stage of production you will be able to make fine adjustments but if your lighting is wildly out of balance it may prove difficult to adjust. It is much better to think before you shoot so let's just recall what the key points are.

**GOLDEN RULES FOR GOOD COLOUR BALANCE**

1) Before you shoot, consider the colour temperature of the lighting in the area which you intend to show.

2) If daylight predominates, match the colour temperature of any tungsten lights you are using by fitting blue dichroic filters to

them. You can use fitted glass dichroics or cut sheets of gel and clip them in front of your lights.

3) If you are shooting on video select the appropriate colour filter for the predominant light source. That is 6500K for daylight and 3200K for tungsten.

4) If you are shooting on film and your scene is balanced for daylight, use daylight stock or use tungsten stock with a wratten 85 filter on the camera lens. If your scene is balanced for tungsten light, there is no daylight and you are not using dichroic filters on your lights, shoot on tungsten stock without a filter.

It may all sound rather complex but you will soon find that the adjustments I have described  will only take you a few minutes.

**WORKING WITHOUT DAYLIGHT**

Let's return to that lady sitting in the window. She is still waiting to blow out the candles on her cake. For a minute I want to you to imagine that the window is not there. In stead of sitting in a window her chair is now against a wall. In this new situation, as you have no doubt already worked out for yourself, you do not have to use dichroic filters on your lights because there is no daylight. You simply work with your tungsten lights, which you now know have a temperature of 3200k. Select the appropriate video camera filter or load your film camera with tungsten stock and shoot without a camera filter and the results should be fine.

**LIGHTING CHECKS**

When you light any scene you should not only try to ensure that the overall colour balance is going to be correct.You should also try to be as creative as possible and make your shots agreeable to watch. Underexposed, badly lit shots and jerky camera movements are unprofessional. It is worth taking the time to get things right. Look for the simple mistakes which can make your work look amateur. For example,in the scene we have just discussed, from your camera position can you see any of your lamps reflected in the widow ? Are there any unpleasant shadows ? Is any one person blocking out another or is anyone's shadow falling across someone else's face ? Is the lighting reasonably even? I am not suggesting it needs to be exactly the same intensity at every point. There should be enough variation and contrast to give a scene shape but if it is too light or if there are any excessive contrasts it may not look right, especially of you are shooting on video. Check the edges of your shot and the backgrounds. Does the lighting fall off in the distance? If the foreground is much brighter than the background, the latitude of the film or tape you are using may not be able to cope and reproduce the scene as you see it now. The background may go black or the highlights burn out. You may need to anticipate problems like that and provide an additional back light or make other adjustments.

If you are shooting with sound and using a detachable microphone, check with the mike in the position it will be in when you shoot. Is it casting a shadow on the subject you are filming or on the background ? You should also check things your audience will never see ? Are the cables supplying your lamps taped to the floor or run overhead or round the edges of the room so no one can trip over them ?. Are the lamp stands firmly fixed or have you failed to fully extend the legs so they can be knocked over by the slightest touch. They are all small points but if you don't check them and someone accidentally knocks over a light which comes crashing down on someone's head your career may be over before it can start.

## SHOOTING IN LOW LIGHT LEVELS

From time to time you may find you have to shoot in places where it is impossible to use your own lights and where there is a very low light level. A few years ago cameramen faced with such situations simply went home complaining that it was impossible to film. They cracked jokes about being expected to film black cats in coal cellars at night and left it at that. Today those jokes are no longer funny for it is technically possible to shoot almost anywhere. Infra red night viewfinders and filters make it possible to film in the middle of the night, as television pictures shot in the world's war zones constantly remind us. Of course, shots obtained in that way will not be of the same quality as pictures which are properly lit. If you are a film cameraman you will describe the results as "grainy". If you are shooting on video the same overall fuzzy effect will usually be dismissed as "noise". For normal shooting there is still no substitute for good creative lighting but you may have to shoot at locations where it is not available and for those moments you should be prepared.

## BOOSTING A VIDEO SIGNAL

Let's consider video first. Modern video cameras will produce acceptable pictures at quite low light levels without using any special infra red attachments. You will find the controls on your camera include a gain switch which will enable you to boost the signal you record by simply moving a switch to increase the camera's sensitivity to light. There will probably be three settings - one for normal light , another which will boost the gain by +9dB and a third which will make it even more sensitive and increase the gain by +18dB. In practical terms, the first setting is the one you will use for most of your filming. When light levels are very low or when you need to select a higher lens stop to get a greater depth of focus (this is explained in more detail below) you will find increasing the gain by 9db gives perfectly acceptable pictures. There will be an increase in the picture "noise" level but it will not be very noticeable. If you select the third position and increase the gain by 18db there will be a more noticeable loss of quality. Equipment manufacturers will tell you that it is perfectly acceptable and that is true when there is no alternative. If you have to get your shots and that is the only way to get an exposure, it's the only method you can use.

## USING HIGH SPEED FILM STOCK

If you are shooting on film and have to work in very dark conditions you will need to load your camera with the fastest film you can get. Film speeds normally range from around 16 ASA to over 1000 ASA. The letters refer to the American Standards Association which sets standards for a number of different motion picture dimensions and uses. The key point you need to know is that the higher the film speed is the more sensitive it will be, so if you are filming in a very dark room without lights you will stand much more chance of getting a good exposure with a 500 ASA film than you will with one rated at 25 ASA.

As with video, as film speed increases definition falls off. A very fast film will be noticeable grainy while a slow speed one will produce images which are clear and sharp. In recent years companies like Kodak and Fujii have done a magnificent job in developing new stocks which give good results at light levels which not long ago would have encouraged cameramen to reach for the nearest bottle to drown their sorrows. You can intercut scenes shot on different types of stock so if you have one location which is very dark you can shoot all the scenes at that location on high speed film and the rest of your showreel on a lower speed stock.

## FORCING FILM

From time to time you may find you have to achieve things which at first sight may seem impossible but even then you may not need to give up hope. As I have already explained, there are very few locations which are so dark it is not possible to get a picture on broadcast quality video. On film, if you have high speed stock available, you can also cope with most situations but there may be a few occasions when you arrive at a location and find the light level is much lower than you anticipated. On video you can cope by using the gain control but what happens on film ? You were not anticipating any dark areas. You cannot use lights and you do not have any high speed film. In this sort of situation you should proceed with the fastest stock you have available. Start a new roll and rate it at a higher speed than the one it is normally rated at. For example if you are using a colour negative which is normally rated at 250 ASA, re-calculate your exposures as it the film were rated at twice the normal speed - ASA 500.

## PROCESSING FORCED ROLLS

When you send the film off to the processing laboratory tell them what you have done and ask them to extend the development of the film. They will ensure that it passes through the processing tanks at a slower speed or through higher temperature baths so the film speed is effectively increased. This techniques is known as "forcing" film. It should only be used as a last resort but when there is no alternative it may enable you to capture scenes you could not otherwise obtain.

You will have noticed that I said that if you are proposing to over- rate any of your shots and ask the lab to force develop those scenes, you should load a new roll before you start. The reason for that is really pretty obvious but in case you have missed it allow me to explain. When your film is processed it will pass through the processing tanks roll by roll at a precise governed speed. The lab cannot develop one shot at one temperature and another at a different one. All the shots on a roll must be rated the same, so if you are going to force any of your shots, re-load and make sure all your exposed film cans are correctly labelled . Explain what you have done on your instructions to the lab and make sure each roll is clearly identified with the production title, the roll number and the speed at which it has been rated then you will not have all your efforts ruined because a lab technician does not realize what you have done.

## FOCUS

You may have noticed I mentioned that when your are working at low light levels it will affect your focus and depth of field. Let's now consider that point in a little more detail. To an amateur movie maker shots are either in or out of focus but as a professional you will want to be more precise than that. By using the controls on your lens and camera carefully and by managing the overall light level you can control the areas which you want to be in focus. Exercising that sort of control will enable you to manage your depth of field.

## DEPTH OF FIELD.

Your depths of field will depend on the focal length of the lens you are using, the aperture you set it at and the points at which it is focussed. That will be easier for you to understand if we consider an example or if you carry out a test on the same lines.

Let's assume you have put three piles of books on a long table. You have placed one pile at the far end, one in the middle and one on the end nearest to your camera. You have four redhead lights at your disposal. For your first shot you are going to turn all of them on and point them all at the table. It is very bright and the exposure meter in your video camera tells you that the correct aperture to use if f16. You look through the lens and focus it on the pile of books in the middle of the table. You then shoot your shot, rewind the tape and play it back. You will notice that although you actually focussed the lens to get the middle pile of books in focus, all three piles are actually sharp. That is because, when you are working with the lens well stopped down - that means at the higher end of the f. stop range, (f.16 rather than the lower end like f2.) you will find it is possible to keep shots in focus over a much wider area. You will enjoy a greater *depth of field.*

Now turn off three of your lights and bounce the remaining one off the white ceiling above the table. There is much less light now and the meter tells you that the correct exposure is going to be f.2. Check that the pile of books in the middle is still in focus and re-shoot your shot. When you have completed your exposure re-focus the image on the pile of books furthest away from you. Find the correct point and then shoot. After a few seconds re-focus so the books nearest to you are sharp. Moving focus like that is called "pulling focus". You can now stop shooting and play-back your tape. On this occasion you will notice that with less light the depth of field is very much smaller. You will see how small it is where you have altered the focus on your lens. It is now so small that only one pile of books is sharp at any one time.

## FOCUS & LENSES OF DIFFERENT FOCAL LENGTHS

The focal length of the lens you are using will also affect the focus of the scenes you are filming. If you use a wide angle setting (like 25mm for example ) you will enjoy a much greater zone of sharpness than you will when you are on the long end of a telephoto at something like 200mm. So , by selecting a lens of a suitable focal length, controlling the amount of light passing through it by choosing the appropriate lens aperture and focusing it at the desired point, you can make your audiences see what you want to show them, and control what is in your pictures to a very fine point.

## BACK FOCUS.

Before you shoot anything on video you should check the focussing system on the camera you are going to use. You will recall I have already suggested it is often worth shooting a test before you shoot any important programme. That is particularly good advice if the equipment you are using is not your own. If you have bought your camera and use it every day the controls will be set up to suit your eyes and your normal method of working but if you have hired the camera from an equipment hire company it is quite possible that it will be lined up to suit another operator. Equipment suppliers will always claim they check and line up cameras between their hire bookings but in practice it does not always happen and it is always wise to check.These are the points you should pay particular attention to.

## CHECKING A VIDEO CAMERA

If you are using a video camera, the first thing to check is the condition of the lens. Is it properly seated in its holder or has it worked loose in transit? It only need to be fractionally out of line to put all your shots out of focus. You will find it also pays to check the focus is correct for your eyes. On video cameras the back focus need to be pre-set and if it is incorrectly lined up you will find that when you zoom out you may lose focus.

## ADJUSTING A VIEWFINDER

When you get your camera,switch it on and attach a tv monitor to the video output socket. Set up a light and point it and the camera at a focussing chart. If you do not have a chart, a page from a newspaper or magazine may suffice. Focus the lens on the text and check the distance with a tape measure. Now check the focussing adjustment in the view-finder and turn it until you think the image looks sharp. Check the monitor and see if you are right. That adjustment is provided because not everyone's sight is the same. Some people have better eyes than others and as we get older our vision deteriorates. Hours spent looking at tv screens or writing books on word processors does not help and you are quite likely to find that what you see through a view-finder is different to the same view seen by someone else. You may think it is sharp while others will not agree and unless your camera is properly adjusted for your sight you will not know who is right. So, make that first adjustment. You can then make a second test and ensure the back focus setting is right.

## CHECKING BACK FOCUS

For this test you should select an object which is about two or two and a half metres away. Lock the macro lever on the lens and open the iris fully - that is to the aperture with the lowest f. number - probably f 2 or thereabouts. Now turn the lens to the maximum telephoto setting - that will be the highest figure - possibly 120mm. When you reach the highest setting you will be unable to turn the lens round any further. Now you can focus the object you are looking at by turning the focussing ring. Check the view-finder and your monitor. Does the image look sharp? If it does not check your settings and make sure the lens is properly seated in its mounting. If it is sharp, as it should be if you have followed these instructions, you can proceed to the second part of the test.

Now you can zoom out to the widest setting on the lens. It may be 9mm or 12mm or a similarly low figure. At the end of the lens nearest the camera you will find a screw which can be loosened to allow you to turn a back focus adjustment. Before you touch that screw, look at the tv monitor. Is the image still sharp now you have zoomed out? If it is, your back focus setting is correct and you do not need to make any adjustment. Simply ensure that the screw on the rear adjustment I have just described is tight so it cannot work loose with vibration when you move the camera about. If the image you see is out of focus now you have zoomed wide, you should undo that screw and turn the ring it loosens very slightly until the image is sharp and then re-tighten. Zoom is again and check that the image on the long end of the zoom is still sharp and then come wide once more to ensure it too is now crisp and clear. It will only take you a couple of minutes to make these checks and they can save a lot of heartache.

**PROTECTING THE LENS**

When you are not shooting with your camera you should always keep the lens covered with a lens cap. The surface of a lens is easily damaged and scratches and dirt can spoil the quality of your pictures. It's a good idea to keep a clear glass filter permanently fitted. It is much cheaper to replace if it becomes damaged. Before you start shooting each day,clean the lens and the view-finder with a soft anti-static cloth. If you do not check and there is a speck or a smear you have not detected it may appear on every shot.

Your video camera view-finder will probably have several other controls. There will be a brightness adjustment and controls which will enable you to adjust the peaking and contrast. Those controls will only affect the image in the view-finder but again they will help you to obtain an image which suits your sight and which you will find is agreeable to work with. You can line up the view-finder by selecting colour bars on the camera before you start to shoot.

## MOBILITY WITH VIDEO CAMERAS

Video cameras can have their own on board recorders. One of the advantages of modern systems like Betacam SP is that they are self contained. The cameras will work, and indeed are normally used, with their own on board recorders.This gives you the mobility which for so many years video cameras lacked. At one time the only way to record on video was to connect your camera to an external recorder and that meant having trailing cables which made it difficult to manoeuvre. You can still use any professional video camera with an external recorder but you will find many cameramen working on location prefer to work with the built in equipment which is now available.

## VIDEO CAMERA CONTROLS

The other controls you may find on your video camera are likely to include a VTR on/off and standby switch. When this switch is on *standby* the camera is turned on so you can see through the view-finder but the recorder remains off so there is less drain on the battery. Next to that you will find the gain control we have already discussed and there will then probably be another switch which can be set in one of two positions. On the first position it will probably switch on colour bars for you to line up on. On the second setting it will help the camera to deal with excessive contrasts. That setting should be used when you are filming subjects which are very back lit.

Audio controls on your camera will include a small loudspeaker which you can use to listen to the sounds you are recording or to monitor play-back. The output of that speaker can be turned on and off so you do not accidentally record what you are simultaneously monitoring. A headphone jack is provided for monitoring during recordings. There will be at least two audio inputs which can be switched for microphone or line use. Each channel will have its own level meters and the recording level input can be adjusted either automatically or manually. A time code generator and display will also be provided and there will be a mains input for you to run the camera on mains power if you do not want to use batteries.

**BUILT IN FILTERS**

Up to four filters will be built into most broadcast quality video cameras. I have already explained what the colour temperature settings - 3200K and 6500K mean. You may find your camera also gives you a choice of two other settings - 6500K plus a quarter ND and 6500K plus a sixteenth ND. These are simply additional daylight setting which have neutral density filters built in as well as being balanced for daylight. N.D.filters - the letters stand for neutral density - simply reduce the amount of light without affecting your colour balance. If you are working in very bright sunlight you may find that at the normal 6500K setting a scene is too bright to film with even the highest *f.* stop setting. Turn one of the 6500K ND filters into place and you will find the light is reduced enough to let you obtain a suitable lens setting. The same filters can also help you to get a smaller depth of field if you wish to do so.

The only other features you are likely to find on your video camera are connections for time code to or from outside source, and sockets for a play-back adaptor and a video out, which you can use to attach a monitor if you want to see what is going on in colour while you are shooting or do not feel the black and white image in the view-finder is good enough. Like all video equipment, cameras are very sensitive to dirt and dust and they should always be kept in their carrying cases when they are not in use. Treat them with care and they will serve you well. Bang them about and you will have to deal with expensive repair bills and hours of worry.

## FILM CAMERA CHARACTERISTICS

Film cameras are rather more rugged and they tend to have less controls. They range from small very portable cameras like the Beaulieu or Bolex H16, which enable 16mm film makers to shoot simple productions without spending a fortune, to the Arriflex range of 35mm and 16mm cameras which are used to shoot films of every kind in almost every country. Most film cameras have detachable film magazines which must be loaded with film before you can shoot. There are two sides to a film magazine - a supply side into which you must load unexposed film, and a take up side which is used to take up scenes which have been exposed. The supply side must always be loaded in the dark using either a darkroom or a changing back but the take up side can be handled in daylight until the first scene is filmed. Thereafter it too must of course only be opened in complete darkness or the exposed shots will be fogged.

## USING A CHANGING BAG

When you use a changing back for the first time you will probably find it is quite fiddly working without being able to see what you are doing. You may find it is easier to practice first with a roll of waste stock. You can use any reel of film just to get the feel of working in the dark. Before you load anything which matters make sure the changing bag is spotlessly clean inside and out. Remember even specks of dust can scratch film and make all your work unuseable. So use a hand vacuum cleaner to clean the inside of your bag. Before you zip it closed make sure you have everything inside that you will need to work with. If you are loading that means your sealed can of unexposed film, the magazine with the supply side towards you, and a plastic bobbine for the take up side. You can then get to work making sure that the bag is properly closed before you open the unexposed can of stock. Make sure you get the film the right way round. If you have done a test run first you will find it is easier. The emulsion side of the film should always face the camera lens as it is the sensitive side on which your images will actually be photographed. It will be the duller of the two sides - the cellulose base on which the emulsion is mounted will usually appear shinier. If you are in any doubt break off a small section and hold it to your lips. The emulsion side will be slightly stickier than the cell side.

When you have loaded the supply side of the magazine and fed the end of the film through to the take up chamber, check to ensure the door to the supply side is properly shut. If it is secure you can open the bag and lace the end of the film into the take-up bobbine in daylight. Make sure it is secure and then close the take up side of the magazine. Double check to make sure both sides really are shut. If you find you have not shut the supply side properly and are now operating in daylight you will be unable to use the film you have just loaded because it may be fogged. If you are sure all is well, write the stock type and emulsion number on a piece of camera tape and stick it on the top of the mag so you will not forget what stock you have loaded in that magazine. The laboratory will also need to have that information when your film is processed.

You can now attach the magazine to your camera and check to ensure that the film is running smoothly. If it sounds noisy or if it jams it may be because you have allowed too large or too small a loop . If that happens you will need to go back to the changing bag and make adjustments. When you are confident the film is running quietly and smoothly you will be ready to shoot.

**FILM RUNNING SPEEDS**

Film cameras normally run at 24fps. That is 24 frames per second and it means that 24 times in every second the film is advanced by a claw which pulls it down into the camera, holds it still for a fraction of a second in the camera gate while the exposure is made, and then moves it on. 24fps is the standard speed for cinema filming. 25 fps is more often used for television because it is thought that the extra frame eliminates flicker. Whatever speed you are using it is essential to ensure that film cameras are kept clean inside and out. You should clean the camera gate at least between every roll. Many professional cameramen clean it between each shot because a tiny hair or a build up of emulsion can make a shot unuseable.

**ASSESSING THE CORRECT EXPOSURE**

When you shoot, if you are working on video or on film, you will need to frame each shot so it only shows what you want your audience to see. You will also need to ensure that each scene is correctly exposed. Shots which appear burned out because they are too light, and ones which are difficult to see because they are underexposed quickly identify amateurs at work. If you are to make money as a result of your efforts every shot must be correctly exposed so let's see what you can do to ensure that it is.

Many modern cameras have built in exposure meters which will automatically assess the overall lighting level and give you a normal exposure. The easy way to work is to put your camera on automatic and proceed like that. If you do that, you will avoid many of the most common pitfalls but there a few points which you may care to check. Built in meters can only give you an accurate reading if they are pointed at the exact area you are going to photograph. So, rule one is point the lens at what you are going to show and make sure it is lit and ready for you to film when you assess your exposure. You may think that is terribly obvious and of course it is, but you would be surprised how easy it is to set the lens and then move a light or forget to turn one on when you come to shoot. So check that all the lights are on and they are correctly positioned. Have any of the lamp heads dropped off their target because they are not securely fixed? Has anyone moved a lamp out of line and are they all turned on and correctly filtered? If you are shooting video is your white balance correct?

When you have satisfied yourself on those points you can check the exposure and see what the meter recommends. If your shot includes any very bright or dark areas you may need to set your stop slightly over or slightly below the recommended figure to get a perfect result. See what the automatic setting is, then switch the automatic control off and manually open or close the lens by the whatever amount is required. For most situations the automatic setting will probably suffice but if you are planning to zoom or pan in the course of your shot make sure the lighting is the same throughout. If there is a variation the exposure will be automatically adjusted as the camera moves and that may not be pleasant to watch. If there is likely to be a variation, make sure there is enough light to give you and adequate exposure throughout your move or turn the automatic control off. Let's consider what that can mean in practise.

## AVOIDING PROBLEMS WITH COUPLED EXPOSURE METERS

Remember the old lady with her birthday cake? The poor old girl must be getting very hungry while we discuss all these technical facts. She is still sitting there patiently waiting to blow out the candles on her cake. You have lit the scene and checked your focus and are now almost ready to shoot. You are going to start with the cake in close up and zoom slowly back to a mid shot which includes the lady and some of her friends. You have checked the exposure and lit the scene so it is fairly even overall. You have moved one lamp so it can no longer be seen reflected in the window and you have put an extra back light on a wall so the ladies standing in front of it appear to stand out and do not merge with the background. You have realised that when the candles are lit the cake is going to be much brighter than it is now and have used the barn doors on one of your lights to make the top of the cake slightly darker than the rest of the table. The automatic exposure control in your camera tells you that your exposure for the scene will be f 5.6. You check again with the zoom fully extended so it shows a close up of the cake and find the recommended exposure is slightly lower than it is when you are wide but you expect the candles to compensate. You know the back focus on your lens in correctly adjusted so when you pull back from the cake to a wider view the whole scene will stay in focus.

Now it is time for those candles to be lit. There are a lot of them and the cake looks bright. You check your exposure again and see that all the candles lit the cake is reading almost one *f.* stop higher than it was before. Now, if you leave the automatic control switched on, when you zoom out the lens iris will automatically open up as the camera moves from the light cake to the darker area nearby. If you are zooming very slowly the change may be almost imperceptible but if you are zooming at a faster speed it may not look very nice. So, what do you do? You should switch off the automatic control on the lens and select the aperture you calculated when you took a reading a few minutes ago - f.5.6. When you shoot, the candles will appear rather bright and perhaps slightly burned out but that will be quite acceptable. As you zoom out the iris will remain the same, correctly adjusted for the shot you are going to end your zoom with and all will be well.

So, if your shot involves any camera movements,check the exposure right across the area you intend to show before you shoot. Select a suitable compromise stop and turn off the automatic control so your coupled exposure meter cannot automatically adjust the lens aperture and then you will not get a nasty exposure bump in the middle of your shot.

## CAMERA MOVEMENTS

You can use your camera to pan, tilt or zoom. If it is mounted on a suitable trolley (known in the industry as a *dolly*) you can also track. What should you consider before making these moves and what purpose should they serve? Let's consider each of these points.

Watch amateur home movies and you will often find that move is the operative word. Obsessed with their new movie cameras, many amateur film makers endlessly zoom, pan and tilt. The effect is quite disturbing and after a very short time you long for a shot which will remain still for long enough for you to see what is going on. People often fail to realize that movie cameras do not have to move to produce pictures which do. It's the action which should provide most of the movement - not the gyrations of the cameraman.

Before you make any camera movement ask yourself if the move serves any useful purpose. What do you want to show ? Would the subjects you are considering be better presented as two separate shots ? You will notice I said subjects - in the plural for when you are making any camera movements you need to have at least two shots in mind - one to begin with and one to end. If you zoom from something to nothing in particular it will be a waste of time. You should start with a scene which has something to say, then move and end with another picture which is self explanatory. The only acceptable alternative is to pan or tilt *with* someone or something, holding them or it in shot. So before you pan, plan your shot. What are you going to start with ? Is it a nicely composed shot ? When you pan or zoom are you revealing something or concentrating on it or simply moving without any real purpose ? Where is your movement going to end? How will you recognise the point where you need to stop moving ? Whenever possible every move should be rehearsed. What speed are you proposing to use? Do you want a dramatic whip pan, where the camera starts on one shot and instantly whips round to show another revealing very little on the way round? Or would your purpose be served better by a more gradual movement ? Is your focus going to remain the same for the start, middle and end with the aperture you are using or are you going to need to pull focus as the move proceeds? These are all points you find it pays to consider.

## ZOOMS AND TRACKS

I also mentioned zooms and tracks. You may perhaps think they are much the same, after all you can zoom in and out of a subject or track into or away from it. Zooms are easier so why bother with tracks ? To work out the answer you need to consider the capabilities of the lens you are using. When you zoom in and out you will use a variety of different focal lengths and when you are on the telephoto end of a zoom it will make your picture look compressed. Foreshortening is a characteristic of using the long end of any zoom lens. If you want a greater depth of focus or wish to preserve a wider separation of the subjects you are shooting you will need to use a standard or a wide angle lens. If you want to move in or out you will need to track. For most purposes you are likely to find zooms will suffice but tracks can be rewarding to shoot and their importance should not be overlooked.

## LAST MINUTE CHECKS

You are now almost ready to shoot. You have planned your shot, lit the scene you want to start with, decided what camera movements you require and made sure the exposure is correct and not going to change in the course of your shot. What else should you do before you start filming? There is one other move you should make whenever possible. You should rehearse the shot you are about to take. If your production features artistes working to a script several rehearsals will need to be carried out to ensure the artistes deliver their lines correctly and to work out any movements which need to take place. You will also need to practice any moves the camera has to make. If you do not have any artistes and are not working to a detailed shooting script it is still a good idea to do some sort of rehearsal before you shoot even if it is only as camera rehearsal.

You may not be able to rehearse the action. In the birthday cake scene for example, it would obviously be impractical to ask the old lady to light her candles and blow them out twice. If you did that the candles would not look right when you started to shoot after the rehearsal and the immediacy of the scene could be lost. The magic of the moment would be difficult to re-create. That magic can also be lost if you make a mistake when you are filming and that's why a camera rehearsal and a final last minute check should always be done if you can manage it. When the candles are lit you are going to zoom out. Before they are lit, check that movement. Is the pan and tilt head on your tripod unlocked and correctly adjusted or are you going to find it jams in the middle of your move? When you are wide at the end of your zoom, are you going to see anything you don't want in shot? Are any lights in frame or can you see them reflected in anything which will give their presence away ?

If you are shooting with sound check the mike position. If you are using an external microphone like a rifle mike, your recordist may be hand holding it with a pistol grip or manoeuvering it on the end of a pole so it can be placed as near as possible to the sounds you wish to record. Check the mike positions before you shoot to ensure that the mike does not accidentally edge into shot. Give your Recordist a guide to your edge of frame so he or she knows how close he can go. And watch for boom shadows. It's very easy to check the mike itself and fail to notice a shadow falling across the background. All these points should be checked before you press the button and start to shoot. It may not be easy when everyone is anxious to get on with the party You will often find you have to work fast and above all keep a cool head. Do not let anyone deflect you from making your checks. Before any aircraft captain presses the levers which make his aircraft fly he check all his controls so he know that everything is going to work and he will not have to face any unexpected disasters and you should do the same.

## IDENTIFYING EACH TAKE

Now your first scene is ready to be shot. Your technical checks have shown that everything is correct and the people you are about to film are ready and eager. You should always run your camera several seconds before you cue any action. If you are shooting on film you should aim to allow some blank footage at the start and the end of each shot. That will ensure you have spare frames for joins when you start negative cutting and it will reduce the possibility of any shots on the head or end of a roll being accidentally damaged. On video you need a few seconds of time code before the action starts. You may also find it is worth identifying each take. If you are working on film and shooting synchronised sound you will find it is essential to do so.

You have probably seen a film clapper board. Clapper boards ( which are often referred to in the industry simply as a "*slate*") have almost become a symbol of the industry but they serve an essential purpose too especially if you are shooting on film. As you shoot you need to keep a record of each scene and take. When you are editing the editor will need to know what takes you want to use and he must be able to identify them. When you are on location you will find it pays to keep detailed notes of every shot you shoot. Working on film the camera assistant will normally keep camera sheets which list the slate number for each scene and take and record the footage used for each shot. On video the time code of each scene should be noted. A clapper board held in shot at the beginning or end of each take will help to make it easier to identify. If you have not got a clapper board, writing the scene and take number on a bit of card or even a sheet of paper can help when you are working on video. On film you need more, especially of you are shooting with synchronised sound.

## SYNC SOUND SHOOTING

As you now know, when you are shooting on tape, sound and picture are normally recorded on the same tape alongside each other. On film the situation is quite different. The unexposed film stock you load into your camera will probably be "mute". It may have perforations down one or both edges and it is designed for photographing pictures and not for recording sound. Your sound will usually be recorded on a separate tape recorder like a Nagra. It will record on a quarter inch tape which is locked electronically to the camera by a synchronising pulse which ensures it and the camera run at precisely the same speed. When your have finished shooting the tape will be re-recorded on perforated magnetic film ready for cutting and when that is done the same recorded pulse will govern the speed of the film recorder, ensuring it is the same as your camera was when you filmed - normally 24 frames a second or 25 fps for television. The editor's first job is to synchronize the 16mm magnetic sound transfer with a print of the mute picture. That operation is known as *synchronising rushes* and it cannot take place if the shots and sounds are not clearly identified for reasons which we will now discuss.

## SYNCHRONISING SOUND AND PICTURE

For a minute let's jump ahead. I want you to imagine you have finished shooting your film and are now in the cutting rooms. The film has been processed and the sound transferred from tape 16mm film. You pick up the two reels of film and put them on an editing machine. If there aren't any clapper boards you will soon find you have a problem. You know sound and picture were recorded at the same speed. The synchronising pulse guaranteed that, but how are you going to re-synchronise the two reels of film you have before you ? If you run them side by side you will probably find the sounds do not match. The lip movements of people appearing in the pictures do not precisely match the sounds on the magnetic film. They are *"out of synch"* because they do not co-incide and they will not do so until you can ensure that the sound and picture of each shot starts at precisely the same point. You need a common reference point on both sound and picture. A point where you can put the two pieces of film together and ensure they match frame for frame. Now, if a clapper board has been filmed at the start of each scene and take you will be able to synchronise sound and picture very easily. You will simply need to run the picture down to the point where you see the board and note the exact frame where the hinged part at the top and the main part of the board first meet when they are banged together. Mark that frame with a cross and then turn to your sound. Run down till you hear an aural identification of the scene and take number you can read on the slate in the picture and then identify the one frame where the bang first occurs. Mark it with a cross and put your two crosses opposite each other on your editing machine and sound and picture will be "in synch" and will remain so until the end of that take. Now you will appreciate why clapper boards are essential when shooting synchronised sound on film.

## END BOARDS AND SUBSTITUTES

If you cannot use a slate at the start of a shot, you should always include one at the end of each shot. Hold it upside down so the editor knows it is an end board and does not try to synchronise the wrong sound. If it is a sound take the scene and take number should be called out in the normal way with the additional words " end board" added. When the board has been banged together the camera can be cut and the sound recorder can be stopped. A few simple words like

" Scene 28, take 4. end board" and the sound of the board being banged together while it is upside down ( for the end of the take) can save a lot of time when cutting begins. If you are shooting without sound the board should be kept open without banging the two parts together. Again if it is on the end of a scene it should be held upside down. If you have lost the clapper board or do not possess one, as a last resort get someone to write the scene and take number on a sheet of paper, zoom into a close shot and then get someone to clap their hands together. That, like a clapper board, will provide an easily identifiable synch point.

## SOUND ON FILM

I have said that when you are shooting on film sound is always recorded on a separate recorder. That is the general rule but there used to be a system which allowed sound to be recorded on a magnetic strip on the edge of the film in the camera . That system which was known as *combined magnetic recording (commag)* or *sound stripe* is now largely obsolete but I mention it now in case you come across it on your travels.It was originally introduced for news filming but now video has largely taken over and most commag equipment has been consigned to the bin.

## EXPECT THE UNEXPECTED

When you shoot, you will not find everything will go according to plan. If you have done your "pre-flight" checks you will find have minimised your problems but difficulties may still arise. If you are working with actors they will forget their lines. People will walk out of shot by moving further than they are meant to move or they will take one pace too few and end in a pool of darkness in stead of in the area you have carefully lit. Aircraft passing overhead or people dropping things may spoil your sound and you will frequently find props which work very well in rehearsal have a maddening habit of failing to work during a take. I remember one occasion when a school science programme was being shown live on network television. The programme was presented by a rather pompous professor who seemed to believe that the experiments he proposed to demonstrate were all quite foolproof and could be understood by anyone. In rehearsal it seemed he was correct but when we were on the air, for some apparently inexplicable reason, when he tried to light a gas ring to begin one of his experiments, it would not ignite. For a few seconds he managed to waffle on but as it became clear that the flame on which his whole experiment depended was not going to light, the self assured professor began to lose his calm. After several more seconds he began to panic and several words not normally heard in school programmes filled the studio. As thousands watched, this very experienced scientist's self confidence began to fail him and we had to quickly cue the next scene which took place on another set and cut away from the professor. Unfortunately the next set had been built alongside and, while we could no longer see the professor, his voice could be heard very well indeed. Until someone managed to silence him, sixth form science seemed much more lively that it normally did.

Whatever you are shooting and whether you are working on film or on video, your primary objective must be to get suitable shots and sounds to ensure that when you arrive in the cutting room you have all the materials you need to work with. You will need a lot of shots to produce a lively programme. We have all seen programmes where the producers have stayed on one shot for minute after minute or cut to a presenter or some other "talking head" whenever their visual imagination failed or the budget ran out. If you want a lively showreel and a programme which will do justice to your talents you should make every effort to shoot a variety of shots. Use the creative powers at your command and get long shots, mid shots and close ups filmed from a variety of angles so you can entertain your audiences and not hold them to ransom.

## CROSSING THE LINE

Sometimes every shot you shoot will show a different subject. On other occasions you will find you have to feature the same subject in a number of shots, filming it from various angles which will eventually be edited together to make a continuous sequence. When that happens you will find you need to think very carefully before you take each shot. Continuity will be a prime consideration. Take that birthday party for example. You have now shot the opening shot and the old lady has blown out her candles. You started with the cake in close up and ended with a mid shot showing a small group of people with the old lady in the middle, the cake on her left and her friends standing on her right. That was a nice scene setter but one shot will not enable you to capture all the spirit of the occasion. The cake will now be cut and the party will get going and you must capture that on tape.

The party is just beginning to get underway. If you try to stop it so you can film, you may lose the atmosphere and make the whole scene appear stilted and staged, so you must move quickly. You decide to take the camera off the tripod and get some hand held shots of the ladies cutting the cake and enjoying themselves. What must you avoid ? The first thing you need to watch is the angle you shoot from. In your opening shot the old lady was looking from right to left and your lights have been set with that in mind, so don't cross the line or start shooting from the opposite direction. If you move past the old lady and take the next shot from just inside the window looking the opposite way, when you come to cut your shots together she will suddenly appear to have turned round. Your lights would also be shining in your lens. So keep the overall geography the same. You can get a close up of her smiling face and another of her frail hand trying to cut the cake. Close ups of her friends applauding might also be nice and you could try a low angle mid shot with the cake in the foreground and the party goers behind. Before you shoot each shot check the edges of your frame. Any mike or lights in shot ? Is everyone looking the right way and not peering at the lens ? When you are satisfied everything is in order you can press the button.

## CUTAWAYS

When you are shooting unscripted scenes you should always shoot *cutaways*. The term "cutaway" is one of the most important you will need to know about when you are filming any shots which will eventually need to be assembled as a continuous sequence. A cutaway is a shot which features a subject other than the previous and following scenes but which is relevant to them. It will enable you to cut from one shot to the cutaway and then on to another shot or back to the first one at a different point without the action jumping. For a very obvious example let's consider a football match. Your first shot shows someone scoring a goal and when that is over you want to go and see the teams kicking off at the start of the next half. If you cut straight from the goal being scored to the kick off, the players will appear to jump from one end of the field to the middle without any apparent reason. It will not look good because the move will be un- natural but you can use a cutaway to make it seem acceptable. When you cut from the shot of the goal being scored, simply insert a shot showing a section of the crowd cheering and waving. You can then cut back to the kick off coming into the new shot as the action resumes. You have avoided showing about a minute of inaction and now the move looks perfectly acceptable. There is no jump thanks to that intermediate shot - the cutaway.

When you have to shoot unscripted scenes always shoot cutaways. They can take many forms and they will get you out of trouble on many occasions. At that birthday party, the cutting of the cake could give you continuity problems. If you only have mid shots all showing the people and the cake you will be unable to cut them together because if you do the action will jump. There will be more cut slices of cake in the later scenes than in those you shoot first. By shooting a cutaway - perhaps showing the old lady's face smiling but not including the cake, you can cut smoothly whenever you wish without worrying about how many slices have been cut.

## SHOOTING INTERVIEWS

If your showreel includes interviews, again there are a number of potential pitfalls you will need to avoid. Let's consider an example and you will see what I mean. Imagine you are about to shoot someone interviewing the property developer who wanted to build a supermarket on the site of that cinema we heard about earlier. You have arrived at his office and are about to set up your camera. It's a busy place and there is a lot of noise in the background. Word processors are clattering away and phones are ringing, so give the man a personal radio mike which you can clip on to his tie so his voice can be picked up without too much background noise. When you set up your camera, choose your background carefully and make sure that when you are in close up there are no objects in the background which could look as if they are growing out of his head. Arrange your lighting so the strongest light ( the key) is beamed in from the right and place a filler on the left (or vice versa). You may need another light on the background. Check the colour temperature of the lights . As the office ceiling is full of fluorescent tubes which you cannot turn off, you must white balance the camera to ensure your colours are correct. Now, how can you ensure that you will be able to cut the interview you are about to shoot and use it as you feel it should be used in the final edited version of your video ?

You must ensure you have the right shots to work with. First you should shoot what is known as a "master shot". From your first camera position, facing the man who is being interviewed, if you pull back to the widest point on your zoom you can see the back of the interviewer on the left of camera. You may decide you want to start with him in shot and then zoom in or you may wish to leave him out of shot altogether at this stage. The important thing about that interviewer is that, whether you decide to show him or not, the man you are interviewing will naturally look to whoever is asking the questions when he responds. That will dictate his eyeline. He will be looking very slightly right to left and you should bear that in mind when you shoot any other shots.

First get the main part of the interview "in the can". You can shoot that from your first camera position. It is fairly standard practice to alter the focal length of a shot while the interviewer is asking a question. It gives you more cutting points. If the first question is shot on a close mid shot and the second one on a close up you can cut from one to the other if you want to but if they are both close mid shots you will need a cutaway in between. It is mistake to stay on a wide shot for too long when you are filming an interview. If you do that it will be boring to watch. When you have got the main part of the interview in the can and your subject has answered all the key questions, you can move the camera and shoot any other shots you feel you need.

You have now got a master shot which hopefully covers the main points you want this particular interview to make. You have probably had to shoot quite a lot to get the points you actually require. When you get into the cutting rooms you can use the interview by cutting into and out of it with the man you have questioned in vision, or by cutting away to other shots after you have established who is talking. If the dialogue is relevant, you could start with the interviewee in vision and cut the picture only at various points continuing the interview sound and using relevant pictures to illustrate the points being discussed. We will see how that can be done later. If you wish to use a longer section of the interview in vision, and do not want to insert scenes shot at other locations, you will need to shoot another shot which will give you the cutting freedom you will find you will need. You will require some "reverses".

## SHOOTING *REVERSES*

As I have already said, you may be able to cutaway from your main subject and insert shots filmed elsewhere. That may not be practicable because there may not be any suitable shots available. If you still feel you need to shorten the interview or "telescope" (shorten) part of an answer, you will need to cut to the only other subject audiences will find acceptable - the person conducting the interview. You can show a shot of him or her listening and nodding in agreement or making some other non speaking move (a reaction shot) or you can see and hear the interviewer asking a question or reacting to a particular point. Let's see what you should do to obtain those shots.

When you have finished filming the main interview you will often find the person you have been filming is unwilling to wait while you shoot the other shots your require, so you may have to stage them without him being there. Move the camera to a new position facing the interviewer and select a close up or a close mid shot or a close up. Make sure the eyeline is correct. You are now shooting *a reverse* - the reverse angle to the one you used when you filmed the person being interviewed. If he was looking from right to left when the interview was conducted, your reverse should have the interviewer looking from his left to his right. The eyeline does not need to be drastically different. Don't have him looking at right angles, but ensure the eyelines for interviewer and subject are opposite and at the same height. If they are not, when you cut the two shots together it will seem very odd because both people will appear to be looking the same way and it will seem unnatural.

## TELE PROMPTERS

When you are shooting someone talking to camera, you may sometimes find they want to have the script written down on some kind of prompting device like an Autocue. Tele prompters can be used with film and video cameras. They can be hired by the day and they usually come with an operator who will type the script on a special word processor. A glass translucent screen is then set up in front of the camera. The camera shoots through that screen which does not appear in vision. The subject being filmed can read the script which is projected on the glass so he appears to be looking straight into the lens. The tele prompter operator monitors the reading and moves the script up line by line as the words are spoken. With a good operator and a reasonably competent performer, prompting equipment is fine. From a cameraman's point of view it is easy to use. It will not take long to set up the camera with the extra equipment all around. You can still zoom but you may not be able to pan or tilt. For most "talking heads" that will not be a problem. If you have to move, the prompter can be set up alongside rather than over the camera lens, though that will not look so natural as the eyeline will be wrong. The person speaking will appear to be looking off camera in stead of speaking directly to it. Professional actors will have no difficulty using tele prompt devices but amateur performers may make it extremely obvious that the words are being read. Adequate rehearsal may help to remedy that situation.

## SHOOTING SPECIAL EFFECTS

You may sometimes find you need to shoot scenes which require some kind of special effect. Some special effects, like explosions and crashes, need to be set up by experts. When you are faced with putting the results of their expertise on film there are two filming techniques you may find are helpful - slow motion and the use of a variable speed shutter. Let's take slow motion first.

## SLOW MOTION

If you are shooting on video, slow motion effects can be produced quite easily when you are cutting. You simply replay your master tape on a recorder equipped with a *dynamic tracking* facility. That will allow the replay speed to be accelerated or slowed down. Run a new roll of stock on another recorder and replay your master using the DT control to vary the speed as you wish. You can also freeze a frame using the same equipment.

Working on film slow motion is best dealt with as you shoot. You can employ laboratory processes later by stretch printing your film so every second frame is printed twice to slow the action down. That is what happens when old silent films, originally shot at 16 frames a second or even slower with hand cranked cameras, are prepared for showing on modern sound film projectors. For most film slow motion you simply need to shoot with a camera which has a variable speed motor. You can then run film through your camera at much faster speeds than the standard 24 frames a second. The faster it passes through, the slower the action will seem when it is projected at normal speed. If you want to slow down a golf ball so you can see it being hit off a tee, a speed of around 400 fps will show the club bending and the effect on the ball when it is hit. The important point to remember when you are shooting slow motion scenes is that as your film is moving much faster through the camera the exposure time will be shorter so you will need much more light. For fast camera speeds you will need very bright light indeed and a highly sensitive fast film.

## USING A VARIABLE SPEED SHUTTER

Another control you may find useful if you are doing any kind of high speed filming is a variable shutter. You will find many professional film and video cameras have this facility. To understand how they work you may find it helpful to recall what can happen if you take a series of still photographs of a juggler at work. On a still camera there are various shutter speeds from long exposures of a second or more, slow speeds of a twenty fifth and a fiftieth of a second and high speeds of a thousandth of a second or more. Now if you photograph your juggler with a slow speed like a twenty fifth of a second the picture will be blurred. The juggler is moving fast and the slow shutter speed is too slow to freeze the movement. Take another picture with the shutter set at a thousandth of a second and you will find the image should be sharp. The action has been frozen because the shutter reaction was quick enough to capture it without any blurring movement. When you are shooting on film or video the same principle applies. Most film and video camera shutters are normally set at a standard 50 the or 60 the of a second. That is perfectly adequate for most normal filming. If you are panning with a moving subject it will hold the movement perfectly well but if you want a special effect and wish to slow down or extend the action using a variable speed shutter will enable you to get the effect you require but don't forget to adjust your exposure.

I hope that by now you have acquired enough basic skills to go out and start shooting. You will learn much more when you put the techniques we have discussed into practice. At the end of your shoot you should have all the pictures and sounds you need to turn your showreel into a film or video which will achieve its objective. In the next chapter we will see what you can do with it in the cutting rooms.

# CHAPTER 5
# POST PRODUCTION

## EDITING AND COMMERCIAL SUCCESS

If your showreel is to prove to be a worthwhile investment it must win and retain the interest of the audiences who will see it. Editing will play a key role in achieving that objective. If all or part of the production cost is being met by a sponsor, you will also need to satisfy your sponsor's aims. It is not always easy to reconcile the requirements of a sponsor and those of an audience. Some sponsors, particularly the inexperienced ones, are under the illusion that unless their name or a reference to their services or products occurs every few minutes audiences will fail to get the message they wish to impart. In practice, as you are no doubt aware, the opposite is often true. The more the sponsor trumpets his abilities the less interested audiences become. As a producer you may find you are in the middle of this battle. Your first objective must always be to interest an audience. If you succeed in doing that you will be much more likely to get a job. Your showreel may not itself be a major commercial success. That may not be your aim, but if it demonstrates your abilities as a competent programme maker it should help you to get a job or encourage others to commission you to do work for them .Good editing will do much to help you to meet your objectives

## EDITING - AN AMATEUR VIEW

You have now shot your programme. It is sitting on the shelf either in cans of exposed film waiting to be processed or in boxes of exposed broadcast quality video. After all the work you have done in preparing a script, finding locations and then shooting you may feel you have done enough already. Many amateur movie makers feel that to make a film all you have to do is go out with a camera, point it in the right direction and press a button. You then come back and cut out the blank bits. If only they were right! As you have already discovered, there is a lot of work involved before you can shoot at all and much more when you are shooting and the two most important stages of production are still waiting to be done. You must edit your showreel and then promote it so you can achieve your objectives and in the following chapters we are going to see how that can be done.

## A CRUCIAL STAGE

The next stage of production - editing- is so important that I shall explore it in depth. It is the stage at which a great deal can be done to ensure even the most mundane subject is interesting to watch. If you have followed my advice and covered the subject you have been filming with an adequate number of shots filmed from different angles, you should have the raw materials you need to work with in the cutting room. If you have filmed those shots from the wrong angles and shot your reverses with the wrong eyelines or lost sight of basic continuity requirements this is where you will find out where you have gone wrong. Skilful editing can turn basic materials into very successful programmes. Incompetent editing can waste the results of all the efforts which have already been made, so the importance of this stage of production should not be under-estimated.

## THE RESULT OF BAD EDITING

Last night I turned on my television to view a video cassette which had been sent to me by one of the world's major airlines. I had been asked to review it for a magazine. A press release, which accompanied the cassette, explained that the video had been shot in seven countries with the help of a leading car hire car company. The budget was not disclosed but the number of locations which had been visited and the prestige of the airline concerned suggested that it had probably been substantial and I looked forward to 20 minutes of good viewing. Two minutes into the tape I was already disappointed.

I have always believed that with experience you can get a pretty good idea of what a film or video is going to be like in the first few minutes of any showing. That belief is based on my view that in those opening moments the production team are going to show if they do or do not know what they are doing. They are going to demonstrate the abilities of the camera team, the sound recordists and above all the director and the editor. That demonstration will either make me want to watch or it will provide a warning that the new few minutes are likely to be boring. And that is what happened with that airline video. The camerawork was fine. The video started with a very exciting shot of an aircraft taking off. A camera had been fixed under the aircraft fuselage so the runway passed at speed and, as the plane ascended, its wheels swept up almost touching the lens. Unfortunately much of the drama of the occasion was lost because there were no sound effects . A totally unsuitable piece of mood music was faded in and we were allowed to hear a few bars before we were treated to the first sentence of one of the most boring commentaries I have heard for years. The editor, possibly because he was restrained by a director who clearly did not know what he was doing, held on to that first shot for far too long. At last the main titles appeared. They to were held so long a child of five could have read them twice. We then moved on to see how the airline and the hire car company provided a service to holiday-makers and businessmen.

The shots were competently photographed. Most had been filmed from the obvious angle but a good editor and a director with more ability than the one in charge in this occasion, would have been able to make the scenes interesting to watch by cutting them together in an interesting way which gave each sequence a different mood and pace. The soundtrack did nothing to bring the video to life. There were hardly any sound effects and a commentary which should have ensured the script writer remained unemployed for life. It described what the pictures already showed perfectly well and failed to add a single point.

That video was a waste of money. The saddest point about it was that it had clearly been a major project into which a lot of people had put considerable effort. They were obviously not a very inspired team but the cameraman could have been worse and the locations visited and storyline followed could have worked if the shots had been put together in a more interesting manner. The production could have succeeded if it had been rescued in the cutting rooms but on that occasion it had not. So how can you ensure your production does not meet a similar fate ?

If you are working with an experienced editor you will find the comments which follow will help to explain what he or she is doing and will guide you on any points you need to consider. If you have decided to edit your own programme I hope you will find enough facts to make what is quite a complex job reasonably easy to follow. Let us start by considering what editing involves.

## UNCUT RUNNING TIME

You have now got a number of reels of film or tape containing all the scenes and takes you have filmed. If you are aiming to end up with a 15 minute video you may have two or three hours of material waiting to be cut. The scenes will probably be shot in any order other than the one in which they will occur in your final edited version. If you have shot on film your sound and picture will be in separate reels of film. So what happens next ?

## SEX IN EDITING

The editor's first job is to log all the material he or she receives. In the following paragraphs I am going to assume the editor working on your production is a man and simply say "he" because you will get very bored if I say "he or she" at each juncture, but if you are working with a female editor or are intending to be one yourself, please do not take offence. I am opting for one term rather than the other for reasons of space, not because I have any preference. There are many excellent female editors in all branches of film and television and indeed, as I hope I have conveyed so far, most production jobs can be done equally well by men and women.

## LOGGING RUSHES

The first stage of editing is to log all the material you have shot. On tape that means running through each reel of tape and noting the time codes of the beginning and end of each scene and take with a brief description of what it shows. On film you should run through and note the slate numbers ( on the clapper boards) and the edge numbers on the side of the cutting copy. Add a brief description and note if the take is with sync sound or mute. You may think it is a waste of time logging what you already think you know very well. You have lived with this production for so long you feel you know it inside out. In fact, though you know what each shot contains, you will not know the time codes or edge numbers and you will find it is helpful to do so as work proceeds. For example, if you are cutting on tape and you want to find a particular shot, if you know the time code of the point at which it starts you can run down to it at speed. If you do not know it, you may have to view numerous other shots as you run through and try to find it.

Working on film you will need to locate individual shots at various stages of editing. When you need optical effects like dissolves or fades or wish to superimpose titles you will need to be able to identify the master film of the shots involved. If you have logged the edge numbers of every scene you have shot, you will be able to find anything quite easily. So, though it may seem a bore going through all your material before you start to cut, you will find it saves time in the long run.

When you have a list which will enable you to find any shots you require without wasting time you can start the work of editing. You may find it helpful if I summarise the jobs which have to be done from the moment you finish shooting up to the time when you are able to show the first copy of your final edited version. We will then consider each stage in turn. The main stages are :

## VIDEO POST PRODUCTION - THE MAIN STAGES

1. *Make safety copy of master tapes*
2. *Produce off line copy with burned in time code for editing.*
3. *Log all scenes and takes.*
4. *Make 1st assembly*
5. *Fine Cut and match master on line.*
6. *Track lay on video tracks and multi track* **
7. *Record any commentary* **
8. *Dubb final soundtrack* **
9. *Title*
10. *Produce final copies from edited master tape.*

\*\* These sound stages of editing can be done at various stages of the work and in a number of different ways as we will see in this chapter.

## FILM POST PRODUCTION - THE MAIN STAGES

1. *Laboratory processes camera original (your master) and prints rush copy for editing. (The rushes or dailies in the USA, which become your cutting copy or work print.*
2. *Master tape sound is re-recorded on perforated magnetic film.*
3. *Synchronise sound and picture rushes*
4. *Log rushes*
5. *Break down shots and hang in bins*
6. *Make first assembly of sound and picture.*
7. *Order any optical effects /titles*
8. *Track lay to augment existing soundtracks*
9. *Record any commentary required*
10. *Dubb final soundtrack*
11. *Match uncut master to edited cutting copy (negative cutting)*
12. *Laboratory grades ("timed" in USA) matched master and produces first show print.*

## WHY COPY UNCUT MASTER TAPES ?

Let's consider these processes in more detail. We will take video editing first. You will have noticed that I have suggested you should make a safety copy of all your master tapes. It will cost very little to make duplicate copies of everything you have shot and very much more to have to re-shoot anything you might lose. Perhaps your material could never be replaced. Even interviews can be difficult to re-shoot as people seldom express themselves the same way twice unless they are working to a script. In any event the possibility of having to re-shoot anything is one you, in common with other professional producers, will want to avoid. If you make a safety copy of all your master rolls you will be much safer than if you simply trust to luck that all will go well throughout the editing process.

Tapes, like film, are vulnerable. They are sensitive to heat and damp and careless handling can undo months of work in seconds. If someone accidentally leaves a master tape on top of a radiator or by a window in hot direct sunlight you may find the tape will not play satisfactorily or indeed at all. It is easy to drop cassettes accidentally and damage them so they cannot be used. If you fail to remove or press in the security tags which all tapes contain to prevent accidental erasure, a tape may erased by simply pressing the wrong button on a recorder. In a well organised world none of these problems will occur but, like most accidents, it is best to avoid them by taking precautions. The most cost effective precaution you can take is to get your master tapes copied in their uncut form on to other tapes of the same quality. Keep the duplicate tapes at different address and store them in suitable conditions. Avoid excessive heat or cold and humidity. If you store them elsewhere, perhaps by asking the duplicating facility which produces them to retain the copies until editing has been completed, you should be safe whatever happens. Even if there is a fire you will have a duplicate master tape which you can go back to and retrieve the results of your efforts.

The second item in my summary of the main stages of video editing was the production of an off line copy with burned in time code for editing. In an earlier chapter I briefly explained the difference between on and off line editing but now we can go on to explore that difference in more detail. First let's see what editing any tape actually involves.

## FILM & VIDEO EDITING COMPARED

When you edit a film, you physically cut the film stock itself and join the scenes together using either film cement or a special adhesive tape. We will consider that process later. When you edit tape you do not physically cut it at all. You *transfer* by re-recording from one tape to another. You replay your master tape on a replay machine and record the section you have indicated you wish to use on a separate recorder. The tapes remain in one piece with no physical damage at all. Working like that, as you will already have realised, you have to go one stage away from your original master tape thus losing one generation of quality. If you are working on a broadcast quality format that loss will probably not be noticeable and if you are using a digital system it certainly will not. If you have decided to economise at all costs and are have shot on domestic VHS tape you will immediately notice the loss.

## ON LINE EDITING - THE BASIC PRINCIPLE

If you decide to work on line you will normally work in a video cutting room - usually referred to as an edit suite. The equipment it contains will vary from one company to another depending on the degree of sophistication required but there are a number of key items you will find in virtually all on line edit suites. There will be at least two replay videotape machines and one edit recorder. One or more of the replay machines may be equipped with dynamic tracking enabling you to play-back at normal speed or in slow motion or to freeze a frame without blurring it. The output of the replay machines will normally be fed via various electronic equipment like time base correctors, which will electronically enhance the quality of the image when it is copied, to an edit controller. That is basically a keyboard into which you must type your editing instructions.

You decide what shots you want to use and, by typing instructions into that keyboard, indicate where you want to come into and go out of each shot in terms of sounds and picture. You can also indicate any effects you require. Do you want to cut, or use an optical effect like a fade or dissolve ? We will take a more detailed look at how you can use an edit controller as this chapter progresses.

The signals from your edit controller, cued by your keyboard entries, will be used to synchronise and co-ordinate the actions of the two replay machines and the edit recorder. If you have entered the right instructions and the tapes all have time codes they will all start and end at the points you have determined and an edited copy of what you have asked for will be recorded on a new roll of tape on the edit recorder. That tape will be your *edit master.*

## ANCILLARY ON LINE EQUIPMENT

In addition to the edit controller, one video recorder and at least two replay machines you may also find the equipment in an on line edit suite includes a sound mixing channel which will enable you to select which soundtracks you use and to mix them together. There will probably also be a caption generator which will enable you to produce captions on plain backgrounds or titles which can be superimposed.  There is also likely to be a some kind of special effects generator. That can vary from a simple vision mixer which will enable you to select a number of simple shapes for superimpositions and wipes to the sort of highly complex machine used to produce ingenious electronic effects for pop videos.

## THE COST OF WORKING ON LINE

The equipment I have described will enable you to produce a broadcast quality edited tape ( your edit master) in one stage and to view every final effect as work proceeds. Working on line throughout is the ideal way to edit any programme but it is not the most common way of doing it because it is very expensive. Editing a 15 minute programme from rushes to show copy on film or on tape can take several weeks and the cost of hiring on line edit suites is high simply because the equipment provided is expensive to buy and to keep up to date. Most on line editors are also well paid because their work calls for experience and skill. For those reasons many people editing on video decide to do most of their work off line and only go on line for the final stages, so let's see how that works.

## OFF LINE - THE BASIC PRINCIPLES

When you work off line you spend most of your time working with simpler and less expensive equipment, and that is where that time coded copy I mentioned earlier comes in. An off line edit suite normally consist of one or two replay machines of a fairly simple nature which are electronically controlled by a relatively unsophisticated edit controller. The controller also governs an edit recorder. The machines involved can be U-Matic high or low band or even standard VHS because the quality of the edited tape you are working with at this stage is not a prime concern. It's content is important but the quality of the image does not much matter because of the procedure you will follow if you are working off line.

The normal way to edit off line is to arrange for all your master tapes to be copied on to whatever off line format you decide to use - probably either U-Matic or VHS. You should ask for the time code on the master tapes to be "burned in" when the copies are produced. Burning in a time code simply means superimposing it in a box at the bottom of the picture. Off line like equipment, like low band U-Matics and standard VHS, does not usually incorporate time code readers and indeed it is not normally possible to record a time code on either of those formats so in an off line suite you will not have the sophisticated time code facilities you will have in an on line suite. The time code on the original tapes needs to be burned into the picture area on the copy you will use for editing. That does not matter because when you have finished your off line edit and have arrived at an edited version which runs for the right time and has the shots in the right order and edited at the correct points, that tape can be sent to an on line suite with detailed instructions referring to those burned in time codes. An on line editor will then match the master tapes to your off line edited copy. He will do that by typing the burned in time code numbers identifying each of your edits into an on line edit controller. Matching (or conforming as it is often called) on line is a relatively quick process. It takes hours in stead of days and the cost is thus reduced. As you are going back to your master tapes for the final stage, and making a broadcast quality copy of them, you will end up to the quality you require without having incurred all the costs of working on line for weeks.

So off line editing is cheaper than working on line. It is less creative short term because you cannot immediately see the results all the effects you wish to see in your final version, but if you work in the manner I have described, using off line for all but the final stage, you will make substantial savings and still end up with a broadcast quality edit master from which superb quality copies can be produced. Again we will explore all these processes in depth in this chapter.

## CUTTING ON FILM - THE BASIC PRINCIPLES

If you have shot your programme on film you will be unable to start editing until the laboratory has processed the film exposed in the camera ( the master) and printed a copy for you to edit. The master sound, which will probably have been recorded on quarter inch tape if you are working on a tv programme or a documentary, will have to be transferred ( re-recorded) on to perforated magnetic film. If you have shot on 16mm stock the tape will be re-recorded on 16mm perforated magnetic stock. If you have shot on 35mm you will probably wish to edit with 35mm soundtracks.

I have said that the master sound will probably have been recorded on unperforated quarter inch tape and for most productions shot on location that is right. If you are involved in a studio based production it is possible the master recording will have been made straight on to perforated magnetic film. In that case you will still be well advised to make a copy, protecting the master recording as you will the camera original and not using it for editing.

## WHY NOT CUT THE MASTER ?

You may be wondering why you cannot immediately edit your master film and cut out the costs involved in copying it. It may sound like an attractive proposition but it would be a short-sighted economy and a disaster in the long run. When you edit, your film will be handled by a number of people at various stages of the work. Wax pencils will be used to mark cutting points and the film will be dragged into and out of bins and through a variety of editing machines. It will inevitably get scratched and show signs of wear. Now if you make your copies from that edited cutting copy - and that is what you would have to do if you edited the master itself because there would not be any other copy - all the damage will be reproduced on every copy. It is much better to ask the laboratory to prepare a rush print which you can use for cutting. When you have perfected your final version your master can be matched to it and copies without joins dirt or scratches can be produced for general showing.

If you are editing on film you will find you need to work closely with a laboratory at several stages of the work. Unlike video editing, where most of the effects you require can be produced either directly on the equipment you are using or later on line by following the edits indicated by your time coded copy, many film effects have to be produced by photographic processes which can only be done under controlled conditions in a laboratory. The superimposing of titles and optical effects like fades, dissolves and wipes for example must all be made in a lab but the lab will take its instruction from the editor so both must work together to ensure the end result is the one which is required.

When the first copy of your un-edited reels of picture has been printed and the master sound has been transferred, the first stage of editing will be to synchronise the two pieces of film so you can view what you have shot. The rushes can then be logged and the main cutting can begin. As I have already mentioned editing film, unlike tape, is a physical process. When you have decided which takes of each scene you want to use, you must break down the rushes into individual shots and hang sound and picture in special bins which are known as trims bins or cuts racks. You can then re-assemble the shots in the correct (script) order. A first assembly is not always very exciting to watch. You may simply cut off the slates and get shots down to roughly the right length. When that has been done you can run through again and make a fine cut in which every shot is cut at precisely the right point to make the film interesting to watch and, as we will see, one or two frames can make a difference between a good cut and one which is disturbing to watch.

The next stage of film editing involves preparing a soundtrack. If your whole film has been shot with synchronised sound that may simply mean cutting the tracks which have already been recorded. If some scenes have been shot mute or if there is no sound at all you will have to provide it. Even if there is some synchronised sound you may find the tracks you have will need to be augmented to bring scenes to life. You may need to prepare additional music or sound effects tracks or a voice over commentary, all of which can eventually be taken into a dubbing theatre and mixed together to make a final mix master soundrack. The process of editing a soundtrack, which is known as track laying, is one of the most enjoyable and creative stages of film editing. We will see how it should be done later in this chapter.

When picture editing has been finalised and all your soundtracks have been cut to match the edited picture, you can go off to dubb a final soundtrack. In the last stage of film editing numbers on the edge of your master film and on the cutting copy made from it will be used to match the camera original to your final edited cutting copy. The final mix soundtrack can then be re-recorded so it can be printed alongside the picture and final copies ready for showing can then be produced.

By now I hope you are beginning to realize, if you did not already know, that editing is a major stage of production and one which is crucially important. It requires a lot of different skills and involves so much more than simply cutting out the bad bits and joining different rolls together. It can be great fun and very creative. To fully appreciate what is involved and help you edit your showreel we are going to consider a number of examples so we can see what you will need to do at every stage. Much can only be learned in practice but if we look at the basic techniques involved I think you should be able to glean enough information to conduct your own practical experiments. By combining them with the advice contained here you will probably find you know enough about editing to put together your first showreel.

## CUTTING WITHOUT A SCRIPT

To see what is involved in editing a simple documentary I am going to ask you to recall a subject we considered earlier - the video about that cinema  someone wanted to demolish and replace with a supermarket. Let's assume you are making that video. It has been shot and is now sitting on the shelf in the cutting room. We are going to see what is involved in editing the opening sequence first on video and then on film.

I am going to assume you have shot this video without a detailed shooting script. In stead of scripting every shot and specifying every camera angle you researched the subject and made a detailed list of the locations you wanted to film at and what you wanted to show on each occasion.  You also identified the key people you felt you needed to interview. You then visited each location and made arrangements to film and subsequently confirmed those arrangements in writing. In the early stages of planning you had to decide whose eyes you were going to use to present your video through and you decided to take the viewpoint of the old man who has been a projectionist in the cinema for most of his working life. Over the last few weeks you have got to know him pretty well. You have also met and interviewed the property developer who is trying to buy the site. Now you have to present both those peoples views to your audience. They have told you what they think and you have got their views on tape but you can put their arguments across in a number of different ways depending on how you use the scenes you have shot in the cutting room.

## ENCOURAGING AUDIENCES TO WATCH AND LISTEN

Your first job is to introduce your subject to your audience and you must do that in a way which is going to encourage them to watch the rest of your programme. You could start with some shots of the outside of the cinema and then show an architect working on plans for the new supermarket, with a voice over commentary briefly explaining what the dispute (and your video) is all about. That would be perfectly acceptable but rather dull and I am going to assume that you have decided to take a different approach. You feel your audiences are going to be more interested in the characters of the people involved than they are in any voice over narrator so you have decided to let the two leading characters - the projectionist and the developer - tell your story in their own words with a minimal linking commentary. To make that work you know you are going to have to use some interviews in vision and to overlay comments taken from interviews over other scenes. You are going to need to use a range of creative skills.

You have shot just over two hours of tape. Much of the material consists of interviews. You soon discovered that filming people who are not professional actors is not always straightforward. It took quite a long time and more tape than you would have wished to get the old projectionist to relax and forget he was being filmed and it took nearly half an hour to get the developer to stop talking in the terms he uses for press releases and give candid views which were obviously his. You also shot the interior of the cinema from every angle and filmed the projectionist arriving for work and doing his job. You have shot other scenes too but for the opening you have decided that those I have already mentioned are the ones you want to work with.

## PLANNING A SEQUENCE

You have decided to start with a shot of the old projectionist arriving for work. He gets there on the bicycle which he has used for over thirty years, and he chains the bike up alongside all the modern cars in the cinema car park. You have filmed him arriving and  followed him into the cinema and up to the old projection room where the equipment is almost as old as he is. You want to start with those shots. For your soundtrack you have decided to use the natural sound effects you recorded when you filmed and to overlay carefully selected sentences from the interview you did with the old man. You are not going to show him talking to camera. In stead you will see him arriving and hear his voice speaking his thoughts. He will set the scene and tell your audience what your programme is all about.

You are then going to cut to a brief excerpt from your interview with the property developer. The contrast will be good. He is a much younger man and the office he has been filmed in is very modern. His views will also provide a direct contrast. You have studied your tapes and identified the section you want to use. After those words you will cut to a general view of the cinema, superimpose your main titles and add some music.

Now you have worked out your plan you can summarise it in a script format before you start to cut:

*1. Ext day. Cinema Car Park. L.S.Tom arrives on his bike and chains it to railings. CAMERA TRACKS BACK as he takes off his cycle clips and walks past the modern cars away from camera towards the old cinema.*

*TOM ( Wild)*
*I've been doing this job for over forty years and I don't know what I'll do without it.*

*CUT*

*2. Ext Car park,day. CMS.TOM approaches . CAMERA PANS with him as he enters the cinema via a back door.*

*TOM (WILD) You get used to things don't you. It's not just a job. I need it and they need me. The whole town needs this place.*

*CUT*

*3. Int Empty cinema.CMS. TOM enters via an emergency exit. CAMERA TRACKS BACK to L.S. showing the whole of the ground floor and the proscenium as TOM walks to the back and exits. It is a magnificent building*

*TOM:*

4. CMS *Gilded figures on proscenium arch.CAMERA TRACKS INTO C.U*

I remember when it opened.It was the Queen mum that did it. She was just a young princess then.

CUT

The man who built it had worked on Buckingham Palace. You don't get craftsmen like that any more.

CUT

5. CU. *Int Projection box. Tom Enters. CAMERA TRACKS BACK with him revealing old projectors and cans of film. TOM walks up to one projector and turns it on. There is a flash of of bright light and he turns to look through a projection port to the empty auditorium below.*

TOM (WILD) The trouble is no one appreciates things like this nowadays and they won't, until they find they can't replace but then it'll be too late.

CUT

6.*Int Auditorium. One person enters and takes a seat. The plush red curtains rise and CAMERA TRACKS into CU of screen.*

DISSOLVE

7. *Int. Office Day.*
*JEFF EADY talks to camera*

*EADY:*
*The people in*
*this town talk a lot of*
*sentimental rubbish. They*
*say they want a cinema*

*SUPERIMPOSE TITLE:*
*Jeff Eady*
*Property Developer*

*but they don't use it.*
*What they really want*
*is a modern supermarket*
*which will make shopping*
*easier for everyone.*
*We've spent a lot of money*

*FADE TITLE*

*on this project and I'm*
*damned if I'm going to*
*let it slip now.*

*CUT:*

8.*Exterior Day. LS. Copper*
*dome on top of cinema*
*CAMERA TRACKS BACK TO D.S*
*showing whole building and*
*area it is in.*

*SUPERIMPOSE MAIN TITLE:*
*LAST HOUSE AT THE GAIETY ?*

*TITLE MUSIC*

---

## PREPARING YOUR EDIT MASTER

You have decided what you want to do
and sitting in the shelves in the cutting room you have all the
materials you need to do it, so where do you start? First I am

going to assume you are working on video. You have made a safety copy of your tapes and have checked that the safety tabs in the master tapes are all either removed or pushed in so the recordings cannot be accidentally erased. You are now almost ready to start to edit. Before you can do any creative editing you will need to lay down a time code on a new blank tape. Take a new cassette and put it on the recorder. Switch the recorder to "manual" and press the buttons you need to press to select time code, video and each of your tracks. Zero the time code counter. Select black on your special effects generator and then press play and record simultaneously on the recorder. Let it run until it reaches the end of the tape so it has a continuous time code and black picture area throughout. You can then switch the recorder back to "remote" and start to edit.

**IDENTIFYING YOUR MASTER TAPE**

You should start by recording at least 30 seconds of colour bars on the picture and the same amount of thousand cycle tone on each of your soundtracks. That is what is known as a "line up". It will ensure that you can set the same level every time you replay the tape and, if it is copied by a video duplicating facility, they will set up their machines to meet those levels so your soundtracks will not be over or under recorded and the video level will be right.

You should also identify the tape with your name or production company in case the cassette is mislaid. The normal way to do that is to use a VT clock. If you do not have one you can shoot any clock with a large second hand and superimpose your name from a caption generator. You will find a clock will be extremely useful when you have to synchronise two or more tapes later in production. Run the clock for around 20 seconds and cut to black and out of your tone three seconds before a second minute starts. You should then leave three seconds of mute black before you start the main part of your video.

## YOUR OPENING SHOT

In the example we are considering your first shot shows old Tom arriving and parking his bike in the cinema car park. From your log sheets you can find which tape roll that shot in on. Put the appropriate tape in one of your video players and run down to the time code where the take you want starts. Now you can see the value of logging rushes. In stead of having to run through every shot on the roll to find the one you want, you can see from your sheets where it begins and ends and wind down at speed. When you reach that point play the take through and make sure it is the one you want to use. You can then identify the exact point at which you want the shot to start in your edited version.

The shot actually shows a lot more than you want your audiences to see. You have started to film several seconds before Tom came into view and there are some kids looking at the camera. You wait till they have gone and then Tom comes into view. As he slows down the camera starts to track back with him. He then stops, parks his bike and moves past some cars towards the cinema. Where are you going to cut in and out of that shot ?

If you cut in when the camera is already tracking back it may look untidy. Try cutting in just before the camera starts to move. Hold the shot as he chains up his bike and let the camera pan round. Hold that shot for a couple more seconds and then cut to the next one, which shows Tom approaching. When you cut those two shots together you will have to match the action of the outgoing shot and the incoming one. Tom is featured in both scenes. You must make sure that he is in the same position when you cut into shot two as he was at the end of shot one or the action will jump. In particular you must match the movements of his feet. If his right foot is on the ground and the left knee is bent on the frame where you cut out of one you must run down shot two and match the same feet positions. The cut should then appear smooth and it will not jump. You need to be precise. If you are even one frame out it will not look right, so pick every cutting point carefully. You can then programme the edit controller to make the cuts for you.

## USING AN EDIT CONTROLLER

The keyboard of your edit controller will allow you to identify the source of each shot you are using and explain how you want it to be used. You can instruct it to make a straight cut with sound and picture being edited at the same point. Alternatively you can tell it to cut the picture at one point and the sound at another. You can specify if you want to cut picture and sound or just picture or simply one of your soundtracks. You also explain if you want your edited sound to be recorded on one or both the available tracks of your edit recorder.If you are working with a linked multi track tape recorder your choice will be even greater for you will be able to specify which of a number of tracks at your disposal you want to use for every sound you record.

You can enter your instructions by using a number key pad and typing the time code of the exact frame you want to start and end on, or you can run down to that point and simply identify it and the machine it is on and press "enter" for each command you wish to make. You will find your controller includes a variable speed shuttle which will enable you to move tapes forwards or backwards at normal speed or at faster or slower speeds or to inch them frame by frame. That control will be crucial in identifying the correct frame on which to cut. So let's see what you should do to make those first edits.

Your original master tape showing Tom arriving on his bike is now on player 1. You intend to start with that shot but there is another decision you must make before you programme your edit controller. Are you going to cut straight into that shot it or fade it in from black ? As it is the first shot in your video it will probably look neater if you fade it in so you should programme your edit controller accordingly. To fade in from black and get that first shot on the screen this is what you need to do :

## CHOOSING THE RIGHT EDIT MODE

## ASSEMBLE OR INSERT ?

First you must select your edit mode. The controller will offer you two different types of edit - insert or assemble. Insert editing allows you to cut into any part of a master tape providing it has a control track and a time code already recorded on it. You have already done that using the techniques described above. Before you use any blank tape for insert editing signals should always be recorded on the video track (it's sometimes referred to as pre-striping the tape). If you do not pre-record those signals it will be impossible to make an insert edit. Insert is the mode you will use for most of your edits. You must also tell the edit controller if you wish to cut just the picture (video) or video and one or more tracks of sound. For the moment just press video and we will return to the sound possibilities when we have made the first picture cuts.

"Assemble" mode allows you to record selected portions of a programme on to a blank tape which has not been pre-striped. When you use the assembly mode all the video signals and soundtracks on the tape you are copying are re-recorded on your new tape. For most creative editing you will find insert is the mode you will use the most and that is the mode to select for the edits we are discussing here.

**SELECT EFFECTS TYPE**

You must now tell the controller how you want to move from shot to shot. You can cut, making an instant transition from one scene to another. You can fade one scene out and another in or dissolve from one to the other either quickly or slowly. Alternatively you can wipe, gradually replacing one scene with another and incorporating a visual effect as the transition is made. In this instance you want to fade in from black. In video editing terms you need to identify that as dissolve in from black. The controller will then ask you to specify the sources of your shots. First it will ask you - *"from"*? You should identify the source of the shot you are coming out of - in this case black . There should be a button for black on your controller keyboard. You can then answer the second question the controller will prompt you with - *"To"*? This is where you must identify the machine which holds the tape of your incoming shot - in this case player 1 - P1 on the controller. The controller will then ask you yet another question - *"Transition"*? You should specify in frames the length of the effect you require. For a quick fade in like this, you may decide to opt for 20 frames. Type "20" on your keyboard and press *"enter"*. The controller now knows you want to dissolve in twenty frames from black to the shot you have selected on player one.

**IDENTIFYING THE CORRECT *IN* POINT**

You must now select your in point on player one and make sure the controller is aware of the point you have selected. If you have not already done so, you should use the shuttle control to wind tape one down to the exact frame where you want the action to start - you have decided that is to be 20 frames before the camera starts to track back with Tom. Mark that as the "in" point on your edit controller. You can the run down to the point at which you wish to cut out and mark that too. You may find it pays to leave it a little over length at this point. You can easily trim it when you get to the second shot.

## SELECTING THE *IN* POINT ON YOUR RECORDER.

The last move you must make is to select the point at which you want the action to start on your new master tape. You will recall that you have already recorded some colour bars, tone and a VTR clock and that you cut out of that clock into three seconds of black. You can now indicate the end of that black section as your new in point. Press the button identifying your recorder and then press "in" when you have used the shuttle control to get the tape to precisely the right point. Now you have told the controller exactly how you want your programme to start. Press "rehearse" and it will show you what you have told it to do. If it all looks as you wish it to be, you can press "record" and the equipment will actually edit the cuts you have programmed. If it does not look right when you play it back don't worry ! Your original master tapes are still as they were so you can try again as often as you wish.

I have outlined the simplest method of entering a very straightforward edit. There are several other ways of doing it  and you will find various other command options on your edit controller, but I think at this stage if I go into more detail it will only confuse you. You will find it is all easier to follow when you have an edit controller in front of you. Use these notes in conjunction with the manual for the type of controller you are using and you should not have too much difficulty in making the edits you require.

## MAKING THE SAME EDITS OFF LINE

The instructions I have outlined above are for editing on line. If you are working off line for simple edits like the ones I have mentioned you can do much the same. You will simply need to stop the tape on the frame at which you wish each edit to start and end and press "enter". If you are editing with only one replay machine and need a dissolve you will not be able to reproduce it on your off line tape and will have to wait till it is conformed on line in the last stage of the edit. You must specify that you want to fade in from black on the instruction sheet you must send with your edited off line tape when it goes to conformed. For the off line edit, just cut in at the point you where you want the fade to be and specify on your sheets that you want it to be a dissolve from black starting at time code 01 04 42 08 or whatever it happens to be. The vital point to remember when you are working off line is that, if you are making anything but a level cut of sound and picture, which can be clearly seen in your off line edit, you must specify what the variation you want is on your instruction sheets.

## CONTINUITY IN CUTTING

You have now made your first edit and faded in by dissolving out of black into the shot showing the old projectionist arriving. You have cut out of that shot as he walks away and now want to cut into your second shot. It shows the old man approaching. So where should you cut ?

Let's look at that second shot again. There is Tom approaching. As he gets near the camera pans with him and he walks away and enters the cinema via the back door.

Now, where are you going to cut? Your in point will to some extent be determined by the out point you have chosen for the first shot. You obviously cannot show Tom in a totally different position or the action will jump. I have already explained that you will need to match his foot movements very carefully. Before you do that you need to check the rest of the shot. If Tom is an open area when you cut out of scene one it will be confusing if he is suddenly seen alongside a parked car when you cut into shot two. So, run the outgoing shot on your recorder and note the salient facts. Now run the shot you want to come into and pick a suitable entry point. Indicate that precise frame on your edit controller and then designate an out point. Choose the type of effect you want to use - in this case a cut. You can then rehearse the cuts you have programmed and see if they look right. If they do, press " record" to make your edit.

**EDL -EDIT DECISION LISTS**

When you have got past the point at which you are intend to cut to your third scene you should again press "edit" to stop the recording. If you are working on line a computer will then store all the information about the cut you have just made. If you want to re-make it or change it at all you can simply call up that edit on the computer and will not have to enter all the information again. When you have finished editing you can print out details of all your edits and produce what is known as an EDL - an edit decision list.

**THE PROCEDURE OFF LINE**

If you are editing off line the basic procedure for lining up the action of the outgoing and incoming scenes will be the same. You should again select your entry and exit points, and use the shuttle control to find exactly the right frame. You can then rehearse and make the edit and press "stop" when you want it to end. Your editing equipment will not be computer controlled so you will not have an EDL and will need to keep comprehensive notes of every cut you make.

## AVOIDING DOUBLE TAKES

Let's consider the rest of the action (picture) cuts for that opening scene and then look at the whole sequence again in terms of sound. At the end of the second shot Tom goes into the cinema via that back door. You must then cut but where should you make your edit ? Do you cut before he opens the door, as he opens it or when he has gone inside and it has closed behind him? Before you can make that decision you will need to check your incoming shot.

Scene three was shot inside the cinema auditorium. It started with a close mid shot (CMS) as Tom entered via that back door. The camera then tracked back with him to a general view of the whole auditorium (LS) Check the start of that shot. When you filmed it did you overlap the action ? If you did you will have taken Tom entering that door and shown it closing behind him in both of your shots so you will have complete freedom in deciding where to cut. If you did not overlap (or repeat) the whole door entry action in both takes, your cutting points will be limited. For example, you may have stopped filming the exterior shot before the door closed or you may have only started to run the camera on the interior shot when Tom was half way through the door. In either of those instances you will have limited your choice of cutting points. Again you will need to match the action so the same events do not occur twice and give you a "double take". You have probably seen badly made films where a car glides to a halt in a long shot and the door starts to open. They then cut to a closer view and the door opens again ! In the example we are considering here you could cut out of the exterior as Tom puts his hand on the door and is about to open it, and then come into the interior as it starts to open. Alternatively you could let him open it and disappear in the outside shot and cut to the interior at a later stage taking care to match Tom's position in relation to the door and the door's open/shut state at your cutting point. They are all simple points but they will affect the professionalism of you end product .

## CUT OR DISSOLVE ?

Your next shot shows a feature of the decor in the cinema itself - some gilded figures on the proscenium. In the script on page 143 you will notice that we have not specified how you are going to get into that shot. Do you intend to cut out of the shot of Tom walking through the auditorium and cut into the figures or would it be more effective to slowly mix (dissolve) from the long shot to the more detailed one ? The choice is yours and again there are several points you may care to consider.

## CUTTING CAMERA MOVEMENTS

If you decide to cut you will again need to choose your out and in points carefully. The camera is moving on both of these scenes. It is tracking out from Tom as he walks back and ending on a long shot, and in the figure shot it is tracking in to a big close up (BCU). If you cut out of the first shot in the middle of the track back and into the figures when the camera is already tracking it, the cut may not look right as you will be cutting in the middle of movements in different directions. If the tracks are very slow it may be alright but, except in action sequences or where you want a cut to be deliberately disturbing as is sometimes the case when you are cutting dramatic scenes, it is usually best to avoid cutting in the middle of pans, tracks, zooms and tilts. That is a general rule. There are exceptions as there are to most rules about anything, but in the cinema example try cutting in the middle of the movements and you will see what I mean. You can then re-programme your edit controller to cut out a few frames after the zoom out ends and in a few frames before the track into the BCU starts. You will probably find it looks neater.

**OVERLAPS FOR DISSOLVES**

If you decide to dissolve from one shot to the other you will need to choose your entry and exit points very carefully. A dissolve is basically a fade out and a fade which are superimposed and which start and end at exactly the same points. The important point to remember is that you will need an overlap. Mark the cut into your first shot. In the sequence we are discussing that will mean marking your in point as Tom enters the cinema. Tell the edit controller you want to dissolve from player 1 ( or whatever it is) to the player which is loaded with the shot of the gilded figures. Specify the length of effect you require. You might choose 2 seconds, which is reasonably slow and for this kind of effect might look right. If it looks wrong you can change it in seconds by entering another figure. Just type 2.00 when your controller prompts you with the word *"transition"*. You can then run the outgoing scene ( Tom walking through) down to the point where you want to start to mix out. Mark that as the exit point for the machine loaded with that tape. When you have done that check that the shot continues for long enough beyond the out point you have indicated. You want to start to dissolve out at that point and your outgoing shot will begin to fade out there, but you have indicated a 2 seconds dissolve so you will need to have at least one more second of the outgoing shot after the exit point as an overlap to create that effect. If the camera stops before that, the effect will not be right and you will have to either enter an earlier exit point or change the overall length of your dissolve. The incoming shot will also need at least half the overall length of the effect before its centre point. When you have checked the overlaps you can mark the entry point for your dissolve on the other player. Rehearse the edit and when it looks right record it on your new master roll.

## OFF LINE DISSOLVES

If you are working off line with limited equipment and possibly only one replay machine you will not be able to immediately view the effect you are creating. You will still have to calculate the overall length of the effect and make sure that enough overlap is available. You can then cut at the point which is to be the centre of your mix. Note the time codes for the overlaps and specify on your instruction sheets that you want a two second dissolve from scene 00 21 55 23 or whatever it is to 00 38 23 21.

## DISSOLVES FOR SCENES SHOT ON THE SAME ROLL

In the example we have considered I have assumed that your outgoing and incoming scenes were shot on different master rolls. In practice you may find that, as they were both filmed at the same location, they have been shot on the same roll. When you make a dissolve or a wipe, to make an edit you must have the outgoing and incoming rolls on separate machines so you can overlap them. If the shots you want to use have both been recorded on the same tape you will need to copy one of the shots on to a separate roll before you can edit. If you want to incorporate freeze frames and various other special effects you will also need to duplicate some of your material before you can edit so it is worth taking another new blank cassette to use as a "dump" tape. If the two cinema shots have been shot on the same roll you can then take your new edit master tape out of the recorder and put it somewhere safe. Switch the edit mode controls to "assemble". Run the blank dump tape down for a few seconds and then play the machine containing the shot you wish to duplicate, making sure it is correctly routed through to your edit recorder so you can record a duplicate copy of the picture, sound and time code. Let it run on for a few seconds after the point at which you intend to cut out in you edited version and then stop the player and the recorder. Take the dump tape out of the recorder and put it in one of your replay machines. You are now ready to make your dissolve. Put the edit master back in the recorder. Re-set the edit mode to "insert"and proceed to make the dissolve using the commands I have described above.

**WHEN TO CUT ?**

There are three more picture edits to consider before we go back and look at this sequence in terms of sound. After the shot of the gilded figures, which you may have decided to cut or to dissolve into, you want to show Tom arriving in the projection room. As you have no doubt already realised, that shot of the figures is a cutaway. It took old Tom several minutes to get from the middle of the auditorium to his projection box and he had to climb up two flights of very dark stairs to get there. When you were filming you decided it was going to be too difficult to light all those stairs in the time available so you shot the cutaway which will make it quite acceptable for your audiences to see Tom in the cinema one moment and then arriving in the projection box. You could make the transition with a cut, without inserting the cutaway if you let him go out of shot in the long shot of the auditorium, hold it for a few frames and then cut to the projection box before or as the door opens. What you should try to avoid is a cut which make it seems as if he is in two places at once. If you cut out of a shot showing him half way through the auditorium and into a shot with him in the middle of the projection room it will seem un-natural and could be confusing.

You can programme those cuts using the techniques we have already considered. Get Tom into the projection room by cutting at one of the points we discussed and then hold the shot as the camera pans with him. He switches on a projector and then walks across to look down through one of the ports. You can then cut to the next shot. Let him move across to the port and look down and the action will naturally lead into the next shot which shows what he will see through that port - the auditorium below, filmed from the back.

In that - the penultimate shot in your opening sequence - the curtains part and the camera tracks up to the screen. You can cut into that shot in the usual way. The next shot shows your interview with the property developer and you want to mix into it as the camera moves into the cinema screen. If you time that dissolve carefully and make the mix a fairly short one, it could seem as if the developer is appearing on the screen. Wait till the track in from the back of the auditorium on your outgoing shot is almost complete and mark a suitable out point. Indicate "dissolve" as your edit mode and then mark your in point for the interview on your other replay machine. Come into it about 20 frames before the developer speaks and see how it looks. If it looks good you can press "edit" and record the effect on your new master roll.

## OVERLAYING VIDEO SOUND

You have now assembled the shots which form the start of your video. We have not yet reached the opening title shot but we will return to that later on. We have also only discussed making action cuts - programmed as "video" entries on your edit controller. Now let's consider the same edits from the point of view of sound.

Many video programmes lack life because the people who make them are so pre-occupied with programming all the picture edits that they forget the importance of sound. Next time you watch television at home turn, the sound off for a few minutes. You will soon feel you are not fully involved. You will also find you notice a lot more about the pictures - how they cut, where the camera movements are and how the overall construction of a sequence works. Sound brings scenes to life and editing soundtracks on video can and should be as creative and enjoyable as it is on film. There are endless possibilities.

## SOUNDTRACKS ON AND OFF LINE

If you are editing on line you will have at least two tracks of AM sound on your edit recorder. You can use those for the first part of your soundtrack and augment them at a later stage by adding more sounds on other video cassettes synchronised to your edit master or by using a linked multi track tape recorder. If you are working off line you will also have two tracks but you will need to log the time codes of every in and out point for each of your sound edits so they can be made directly from the master recordings when your tape is conformed. The tracks on your off line will simply act as a guide.

## THE IMPORTANCE OF BACKGROUND SOUNDS

Sound editing can be great fun and if you do the job properly you can make scenes much more interesting to watch. You will need to prepare several different soundtracks all matching the edited pictures on your edit master and, in the last stages of editing, will be able to mix them together (dubb) to make the final soundtrack audiences will hear. Some scenes require quite complex soundtracks. The cinema sequence we are considering here is fairly straightforward and typical of the sort of work you are likely to encounter editing many different types of videos, so let's see what it involves.

You have two tracks you can use on your recorder and there are two tracks of original location sound recorded on each of your source tapes. You may have recorded the same sounds on both tracks or you may have used them to record different sounds simultaneously. You also have that script which tells us that you have decided to let Tom introduce your video by speaking a few sentences from the interview you filmed with him. You shot that interview in the cinema auditorium, because it was quiet and you knew you could get a clean feed of sound without any unwanted background noise. If you just edit his voice and overlay it over the action shots you have already cut. It will not sound right. Without other natural sounds the car park shots will not come to life so you must use both your tracks to make the scenes seem real. On track one you can lay down your sound effects - the actual sounds recorded when you shot the scenes shown on the screen - Tom arriving and parking his bike, walking up to and into the cinema and so on. When you cut your picture you can simultaneously select "V" (video) and "A1" (Audio 1) when you choose the edit mode on the edit controller. Check the level of the recording and make sure you are re-recording it at a level which not too high or too low. You can make fine adjustments later when you are dubbing. You will then have a basic effects track for your opening scenes on track one of your new edit master. You can use the other track for Tom's comments.

## REPLACING UNSUITABLE SOUNDS

You will sometimes find that the sounds recorded when pictures are shot do not sound right. In the car park shots for example, when you listen to your tape you may find that the microphone has accidentally picked up the voices of people who were standing nearby but who are not seen in shot. They do not sound right and are rather confusing. In situations like that you can replace the location sound with suitable sound effects obtained from discs or tapes, laying them down on your master tape at the required entry and exit points.

## SOUND AND PICTURE CUTTING POINTS

You do not have to cut picture and sound at the same points and indeed will often find it is more effective to cut each in a different place. Sounds, like pictures can be cut or mixed together. Experience will give you a feel for when it is best to cut and mix. For example you may find if you are cutting out of a loud noise into a quieter one at the same location it sounds better to gently mix from one track to another. Lay your outgoing sound on one track and the incoming one on another with a suitable overlap for a mix. Laying background effects can be done in the later stages of editing using additional tracks on other tapes. In the initial stages of editing you simply need to get the essential sounds on the first two tracks of your edit master. In the cinema example I have suggested you should use track one for sounds effects from your source tapes or from a disk or an audio tape. If they are inadequate or too short you can replace or augment them later by adding other tracks. The second track should be used for Tom's comments, which were shot as synchronised interview but which you are going to use "wild" by editing them and overlaying them over other shots.
Let's see what that is going to involve.

## OVERLAYING AN INTERVIEW

If you glance again at that script (page143) you will note that the comments you have decided to use from your interviews with Tom and with the property developer both appear to be very concise. They are expressing views which are clear and which will immediately give audiences an insight into their characters. When you shot those interviews the answers did not seem nearly as clear and it was only when you logged the various scenes and takes that you were able to sort out which comments you felt you will be able to use. You have now got to make those edits and put the relevant sentences on track two of your master tape.

Tom's interview took half an hour to film and it was not easy. He had never done anything like it before and it took you some time to set him at ease but eventually you got him to relax and make some very valid points. You have identified those points and noted them in your script and have now got to extract them from what Tom actually said and edit them to go on your new master tape. With your source tape of the interview on player one you can select the correct edit mode for the recorder. This time you do not want to cut the picture or track one. You have already edited the picture and laid down the location sound effects on track one. Make sure you are not accidentally going to erase work you have already done and see that only track two (A2) is going to be edited this time. You should also tell the controller that you intend to make a cut. You can then run down the source tape of the interview and find the first sentence you require.

## MAKING LONG INTERVIEWS CONCISE

In the interview you shot, as you will now be reminded when you play your source tape, Tom rambled on and on. You do not want to use everything he said. It would be too long and would include a lot of things you do not want your audiences to hear. Let's see what was actually said in that interview. The words you have decided you want to use are in italics.

**INTERVIEWER.** Right. now Tom. I'm just going to ask you a few questions. Just talk to me and forget the camera. How long have you worked here ?

**TOM.** What's that?

**INTERVIEWER.** How long have you been a projectionist in this cinema?

**TOM.** Oh. Ah. That's a difficult one that is. When you get to my age it's hard to remember what day it is. It's a long time I can tell you that. Er. Now let me think. *I've been doing this job for forty years and I don't know what I'll do without it.* Is that thing taking my photograph ?

**INTERVIEWER.** Don't worry about that.You must have seen a lot of changes in the time you've been here ?

**TOM.** Oh Ah! You can say that again. It's changes and more changes all the time now, and I don't like it. *You get used to things don't you. It's not just a job,* Um. Er It's like this you see. *I need it and they need me. The whole town needs this place* you know.

                        With that source tape on one of your players and the point at which you want to start the first sentence of overlaid dialogue already indicated on your edit controller, you can run down to the first sentence in italics, losing all the preamble and the words you do not want your audiences to hear. When you get to - " Er now, Let me think..". You must check and see if there is a long enough pause for you to cut in. Does Tom draw an audible breath?. If he does, can you make a clean cut into the soundtrack after that breath so you come in for the words "I've been doing this job for over forty years"? If you can, mark that frame as your in point and run down to find a suitable out. You want to get out after he says "I don't know what I'll do without it", and you will need to again check and see if there is a pause where you can make your edit. If he runs straight into his next sentence without a pause you may have to reconsider using that sentence. On this occasion we will assume he does not, so you can mark an out point on your source tape replay machine before he asks if the camera is taking his photograph. Rehearse your edits and if they work well, record them. If you feel the words need to come in earlier or later you can adjust the recorder entry points until the words look right when they are viewed with the pictures.

## NATURAL BREAKS

You now have to cut to the next sentence you want to use. Run the source tape down until Tom says "You get used to things don't you". Check that there is a clear frame to cut into and that the inflection sounds right and it does not seem obvious that you are cutting in mid sentence. Then you must decide how much pause you want to insert between the two sentences you have selected when they are assembled on your edit master. The flow of the words must sound normal. You do not want your audiences to realize you have edited them. They must sound natural and to do that the pace of the delivery, governed in part by the pauses you will insert in making your edits, will decide if they do. If you leave a few blank frames it does not matter on this occasion. Your second soundtrack - the one you are using for Tom's voice - will go dead but the sound effects on the other track will cover the gaps and when you dubb you should be able to ensure that the edits pass unnoticed.

## ELIMINATING UNWANTED WORDS

In the middle of the next sentence you want to use, Tom has used some words you will come across again and again when you are editing interviews. "Um - Er" - and "you know". They do not add anything to the meaning of the text and they cause delays in its delivery so you want to lose them. How can you do that without your edits being noticed ?

First check the source tape. Listen for in-drawn breaths and avoid clipping syllables and cutting him off in his prime and then build up the sentence you want piece by piece and cut by cut. Cut in just before he says : "You get used to things don't you. It's not just a job" Cut out just before he speaks the "um and er" you do not want to hear. Make that edit and then run on and find the start of "I need it and they need me". Check that you have allowed enough pause between the outgoing sentence and this one and when a rehearsal has confirmed your entry and exit points are correct you can take that sentence cutting our before he adds " You know". Play back the whole scene and see if it looks and sound alright. If it does you have spent the last ten minutes profitably.

## USING THE SAME TECHNIQUES FOR OTHER SUBJECTS

I do of course realize that you will not actually be cutting the scenes we have discussed in this example but will be editing your own showreel. When you start to do that, you will probably find you need to use some or possibly all of the techniques we have just considered and will continue to consider in this example, so please do not feel it is not relevant to you. Every video deals with a different subject but the techniques needed to make it work are basically the same and with that in mind I think you will find these comments will help to point you in the right direction and save you many fruitless hours.

## EDITING ETHICS

The second interview in the example we are discussing was with Jeff Eady, the property developer. In the pre title sequence you have decided to use a very brief excerpt from that interview and to show him in vision. Let's now consider what you need to do to make that scene work. We will also consider a few general points about editing interviews.

You are only proposing to use four sentences from Mr Eady at the start of your film but in the interview he said a lot more. Much of what he said was pure public relations guff. It took you some time to get him to say what he really thought but towards the end of the interview he lost his cool and became quite angry. You want to use some of the words he spoke at that point. That will not please him became he had spent a long time giving you the authorised version of what he wants everyone to hear, so whose views should you consider? Are you under any obligation to omit words you know he probably does not want you to use? Before we answer that let's look at a transcript of the section of the interview which contains the words you want to include. Those words are in italics.

**EADY.** We have employed the best architects and spent months preparing our plans. We have spoken to all the local traders and are confident they will welcome our scheme which is bound to bring more business into the area.

**INTERVIEWER.** But you are proposing to destroy a beautiful building which no one can replace. Surely your store could be built somewhere else. After all it is just another supermarket.

**EADY**. Look. It's no use your deliberately trying to annoy me. *The people in this town talk a lot of sentimental rubbish.* You and the rest of your media friends have given me a rough time and treated me like shit and I'm telling you now to f*** off. *They say they want a cinema but they don't use it. What they really want is a modern supermarket which will make shopping easier for everyone. We've spent a lot of money on this project and I'm damned if I'm going to let it slip now.*

-----------------------------------------------------------------------

When you edit any interview you are morally obliged to present a fair and honest report of what is being said. That does not mean to have to reproduce it verbatim but it should prevent you from editing the words in a way which makes them appear to mean the opposite of what was said. It is also un-ethical to omit so much of an answer that the portion you use appears unbalanced but omitting the sections you are proposing to lose here is normal practice. It will avoid causing offence, and will be quite agreeable to watch, so what must you do in the cutting room to edit this section?

First you need to run down your edit master tape on the recorder to the end of the last shot and mark the point at which you wish to come in. Select V, for your picture cut and A2 to put the sound of the interview on track two. You can then run the source tape of the interview and find the first words you want to use. After he says "It's no use your trying to annoy me", see if there is enough pause to cut in without clipping the next incoming word. If there is, mark that point as you entry point and rehearse the cut. Check your sound level and if it looks and sound alright you can make the edit.

## WHERE TO CUT ?

After one sentence Mr Eady begins to lose his cool and attacks the media in a sentence you have decided to omit. That could give you a problem for if your simply cut out that sentence and cut in again for the next words you want to hear, a sentence later, unless the camera has moved from a close up to a mid shot or the other way ( which is very unlikely mid sentence and in such a short time) when you cut, the action will jump. So how can you avoid that ?

First mark the in point for that first sentence on your source machine. You have already identified where you want to cut in on your edit master. Run down to the end of the first sentence you require and mark a cut out after the last words you want to hear - "a lot of sentimental rubbish" If there is a pause there, keep it. Now you can make that cut. When you have done that, run down to the start of the next sentence you want to use and mark your entry point on the source machine just before Mr Eady says " They say they want a cinema". If there is a pause there, for the moment keep it. You can now mark the in point on your edit recorder - that will be the point where you cut out just now. Rehearse the edit and see if the pause sounds right. Is it too long or too short ? Does it sound natural or it obvious that you have made an edit? If it is, you will need to either extend or shorten the pause between the outgoing an incoming shots. At this stage the picture will jump but don't worry about that. We will remedy that in a moment. Just get the pause right and check that you have identified the correct entry points and are still cutting V (video) and A2 (your second soundtrack). You can then make your cut.

## ELIMINATING JUMP CUTS

Now you have the words you want to use in the right order and it sounds alright but you have a nasty jump in the picture where you have cut a sentence out. To make that cut acceptable you need to insert a cutaway. When you shot the interview you filmed some reverses so find them on your master tapes. Run down till you find a shot of the interviewer listening or nodding. Change the edit mode on your edit controller so you now only cut the picture (V) and not the soundtrack you have just done. Mark an in point after he has said "sentimental rubbish" and an out point after the words "they don't use it". The picture will then cut away from Mr Eady as he says "they say they want a cinema but they don't use it", and cut back to him as he begins " What they really want is a supermarket..." rehearse the cut. If you have shot your reverses with the right eyeline it should look fine and your audiences will not be aware that any words have been omitted.

**ADDING TITLES**

Your opening sequence is now almost complete. Only the titles you want to include are missing. You want to superimpose Mr Eady's name as he speaks and identify him with the title "Property Developer" That title will need to be superimposed over the bottom of the screen as Mr Eady speaks. It will look neater if it fades in and out, so let's see what is involved in doing that.

Superimposing titles is much easier when you are working on video that it is on film. Using a caption generator you can create titles with a plain background or ones which can be superimposed over the moving shots recorded on your source tapes. Well established caption generators, like the Aston models which you will find in many broadcast television edit suites, have the dual advantages of being reliable and quite easy to use.

**CAPTION GENERATORS**

Caption generators consist of a keyboard which is similar to the ones you will find on any word processor or typewriter, with a number of additional keys for special functions. There is also a computer which memorises information entered via the keyboard and there is a screen which displays what you have typed or stored on disk. Most caption generators will allow you to produce a wide range of different type sizes and styles (fonts). You can create captions with big letters for main titles or small ones for sub titles and you can underline words or sentences and make them flash on or off . Captions can be faded in and out by using a vision mixer or by programming your edit controller with the appropriate  edit modes and entry/exit points. You can also make them roll from the bottom to the top of the screen or across it from left to right or right to left. Your lettering can be tinted to almost any colour and it can be edged with a drop shadow or some other form of surround to help make it stand out when it is superimposed over a bright background.

## CREATING A SUB TITLE

For the sub title we are considering you must first select your title background. In this instance it is a shot of Mr Eady speaking the first sentence you have selected and you will need to mark the in and out points for that edit in the way we have discussed above.  Before you make that cut you can turn to your caption generator and use the keyboard to type the words you want to superimpose.  You may decide to choose one type face for JEFF EADY and a slightly smaller one for PROPERTY DEVELOPER.  Type the words you wish to see, having first loaded the fonts and styles you want to use into the computer from the appropriate typeface disk. When you have got the right words on your screen use the cursor and the arrows on the keyboard to position the lines where you want them to be - at the bottom of the screen. You will notice that the screen on which the letters are displayed has a small area which is slightly darker round the edges. If your letters appear outside that area you will still see them on a caption generator's monitor and on the other broadcast quality monitors in your cutting room because they show the full picture area. Most domestic sets cut off the edges of the picture so to be sure your lettering will always be seen you need to keep it inside the black border on your caption monitor. That shows what is known as the safe picture area. When you feel the type you have set is correctly positioned you can press the "page centre" buttons on the keyboard to ensure the words are correctly centred. You can then return to either your edit controller or your caption generator.

**FADING CAPTIONS IN AND OUT**

If you have a vision mixer, you can use the downstream keyer section of it to bring in the sub title when you want it to appear. Make your picture edit by using the edit controller in the way we have discussed above and use the vision mixer to superimpose the title from your caption generator. On your vision mixer you can set the length of the fade you want when your caption fades in. A 20 frame fade in will probably look right. Rehearse the edit and, when you get to the point where you want the caption to appear, press "mix" on the downstream key section of your vision mixer. The title should then appear. For a fade out press the fade button in the same section of the mixer's controls and the caption will fade out in 20 frames.

**KEYING IN**

The term "key" is the name given to an effect where parts of one picture are used to cut holes in another. In the case we are considering, the caption will cut a hole in the background when it is superimposed so the lettering will stand out. You can key one shot into another. When you watch the evening tv news you will often see shots of events which are occurring elsewhere, superimposed in a small screen above or behind the newsreader. Those shots are being keyed in over the shot of the studio presenter. On a vision mixer the downstream keyer section of the controls will enable you to insert captions or other key effects into your edit master. The controls are fairly self explanatory - each button is usually labelled so you can see at a glance which you need to press to produce an outline and which will give you drop shadow and so on. Outlines and shadows can also be produced on a caption generator. So,first typeset your caption on the caption generator and, when you want it to fade in, press DSK MIX on the caption generator. Press it again when you want the caption to fade out. The background will continue and the title will disappear.

**EFFECTS TYPES**

You can also key in superimpositions by using the edit controller. When you select the type of edit you require you will find there are usually six options. They are :

*CUT.* This enables you to instantaneously cut from one shot to another in the manner we have already discussed

*DISSOLVE.* Cues a gradual transition from one scene to another.

*WIPE.* A transition from scene to scene in which one scene appears to be pushed off the screen by another. You can wipe from left to right,introducing a new scene from the left of the screen which appears to push the old one off to the right. You can also wipe from right to left, from top to bottom or the other way round.

*KEY* Cuts out a section of one scene and allows you to insert another in its place. You can superimpose a caption by keying it over another scene or you can insert one shot into another by using the key control.

*PATTERN KEY* You can use a vision mixer to create a variety of patterns - squares - frames- oblongs - lines - circles and so on. Using the pattern key control will enable you to superimpose scenes which fit the shape of the pattern(s) you have selected. For example, if you have a shot of a tv screen and you want to replace the picture on the screen you can make up a mask using the pattern controls to fit the shape of the screen and then key another shot into that area. When the key control is operated the new picture will appear in place of the one originally seen on the screen. You will thus have keyed one shot into another.

*MANUAL* This will enable you to synchronise two or more source tape replay machines to your edit recorder. Other controls will need to be operated manually from the mixer when it is in operation so if you want to fade you will have to do it manually using the vision mixer rather than pre-programming it on your edit controller. I find the manual control is most useful for synchronising a number of tapes when track laying and dubbing.

**EFFECTS WHEN EDITING OFF LINE**

If you are working off line you will not be able to superimpose your captions during your off line edit. You must note the time codes of the points at which you wish them to fade in and fade out or cut in and out and log them on the sheets you will give to the on- line editor. Spell out the words you want to see on the caption and give a guide on the type size and where you want them positioned on the screen and all should be well.

## PUTTING ADVICE INTO PRACTICE

Now I hope you have got some idea of what you can do using the basic controls in a video edit suite. You will learn much more in practice. The above comments will help to set you on the right course. If you get into trouble you can always refer to the instruction manuals issued by the manufacturers of the equipment you are using to check any specific points. You will find controls do vary from model to model and from one manufacturer to another but the main principles I have outlined, which are based on using Sony editing equipment with Aston caption generators and Grass Valley mixers - a combination you will find in the many professional edit suites - will help you to know what to look out for. Editing is a complex job and much can only be learned in practice but I hope the paragraphs you have just read show what you can do with the simplest materials and a very basic script. An experienced editor would probably complete the edits for that opening sequence in around half an hour.

Let's now see what you would have to do if you had to edit the opening sequence we have just explored on film in stead of on video.

# CHAPTER 6
# CUTTING ON FILM

If you have shot your showreel on film, what will you need to do in the cutting room ? Editing a film is not the same as editing a video. While the basic rules which dictate what makes a cut acceptable to watch remain unaltered, the equipment you will have to use is quite different and the procedures which need to be followed are not the same so let us see what is involved.

## WORKING WITHOUT A VIDEO ASSIST

When you shoot a scene on video you can immediately play back the tape and see what it looks like. On film, as you already know, that is not usually possible. Some modern film cameras have video equipment built into them so a videotape recording can be made at simultaneously .That facility, which is known as "video assist", is intended to be used as a guide to what the scenes contain rather than for making a broadcast quality copy which can be used as a final end product. Video assists are helpful for checking continuity points and for seeing if any unwanted objects are visible in frame. They are also good for checking the performances of those taking part. For your showreel and indeed for most low budget productions, it is unlikely you will be using a film camera which is equipped with a video assist. You will thus have to wait until your film is processed to assess the results.

## PROCESSING YOUR ORIGINAL

If you are working on film, when each day's shooting is completed the camera original (the master) film will be sent to a film laboratory to be processed. You will be dealing with the lab at several stages of the post production work so it is important to choose a lab which has a good reputation. The first task they will undertake is to process the master. The film will be unloaded in total darkness and fed into the first of a series of processing tanks. It will move through those tanks at a strictly controlled speed which will depend on the temperature the tanks are kept at. If development is too long or too short it will affect the exposure so the time your film takes to pass from one end of the processing baths to the other is crucial. If a film breaks while it is being processed all the film in that bath at that time may be lost, so if you do ever damage even one perforation when you are shooting, be sure to tell the lab when you send that reel to be processed. After going through development and fixing baths the master will pass through a series of washes and finally through warm air drying cabinets. The later stages are usually done in daylight. The processed film is then wound on a plastic bobbin and prepared to print your rushes.

## PRINTING RUSHES (DAILIES)

Before rushes are printed, the laboratory will put your original film on a special machine known as an analyser and they will take a quick look at the shots on each roll. If the exposures look fairly even, they will then print a copy of each roll "at one light". That term simply means that, when your original master film is re-exposed on a reel of new stock to make your a rush print, all the scenes are given the same exposure. A film printing machine is in one sense rather like a camera. The exposure it gives can be varied for each scene and the colours of each shot can also be adjusted. Picking the right exposure and colour correction is known as *grading* (*timing* in the US). Most rush prints are made with one overall exposure. It is cheaper to order a one light print than one which is graded. When the programme has been edited, a laboratory technician known as a grader will look at each scene in your cut negative and re-assess the exposure and colour correction it requires to make it fit in well with the shots which precede and follow it. The lab will then use that assessment to print your first graded show print.

When your rushes are printed, the lab will usually give you a report on the condition of the master. That report is crucial because most labs will retain the master until you have completed your editing and are ready for the cutting copy to be matched to it. That is a sensible procedure for your valuable original film is probably safer in a lab under controlled conditions that it is on a van bumping its way to your cutting room. If you need to reprint any shots, the lab will be able to do it for you without any delay and they will also need access to the master when you order your titles and optical effects. So, study that report and see what it says. It will tell you if the exposures are correct and if there is any physical damage to the master film itself. If it is scratched or if a scene has been drastically over or under exposed it will be noted on the report. The lab will print the master on a suitable stock to make a rush print for you to view and edit.

If the lab has a sound department they will also be able to arrange to re-record your location sound (originally recorded on quarter inch tape), on to perforated magnetic film. If they do not have a sound department, you will need to arrange for an audio studio to do the transfer for you. So every day un-edited reels of sound and picture, which have been processed and transferred, will arrive in the cutting room. When they have arrived this is what you will have to do

## FILM POST PRODUCTION - WHAT IT INVOLVES

1. *Synchronise sound and picture rushes ("dailies" in the USA)*
2. *Log rushes*
3. *View and assesses takes to be used*
4. *Break down rushes*
5. *Make first assembly*
6. *Fine cut*
7. *Order optical effects. Dissolves/Wipes/Titles*
8. *Track Lay*
9. *Dubb*
10. *Negative cut*
11. *Produce graded show prints from cut master.*

## EDITING TIME

Film cutting rooms contain a number of specialist machines. You can hire a fully equipped cutting room for the time you require. For a 15 minute film you would normally expect to need about three weeks. An experienced editor cutting a reasonably straightforward film may need less and anyone dealing with a complicated epic will require longer so the time I have specified should only be regarded as a general guide.

## EDITING MACHINES - UPRIGHT MODELS

Now let's look at the equipment you will find in a professional film cutting room. The two main items you will use will be a motorised editing machine and a synchroniser. There are several different types of editing machine. In the USA the trade name of one well known manufacturer - Moviola - is often used to describe any motorised editing equipment. There are two main types - upright and table models. Upright machines, like the original Moviola models, have been used in Hollywood for years. They are ideal for running short lengths of film and for assessing the content and cutting points of individual shots. The picture is driven by an intermittent sprocket with loops above and below the picture gate. The screen is not large but the picture is bright and movement can be controlled by hand or by a foot pedal. Sound and picture can be run together or independently. Upright editing machines, like those traditional Moviolas, can also be used to run rolls of film but many people find table models are more suitable for that purpose.

**TABLE EDITING MACHINES**

On a table editing machine, picture and sound, on separate reels of perforated magnetic film wound on to plastic cores rather than reels, pass from left to right horizontally. On a basic table model you can run one reel of picture with one soundtrack. The drive mechanism can be engaged and disengaged by flicking a switch so sound and picture can be run together in synchronism or independently. On more advanced models you can run one or two reels of picture with two or three soundtracks. Equipment like that will enable you to do many of the jobs you would normally do on a synchroniser (see below) in rather more comfort. Table editing machines like those in the Steenbeck range, are quite easy to use. You can run your film at normal or double speeds or, by using an inching handle, advance or retard it frame by frame. They tend to be kinder to film than upright models. As the film runs from one plate to another, manual handling is reduced and the picture is thus less likely to be scratched. Upright machines have their fans and many editors who have been in the industry for years will not use anything else. Others will tell you there is nothing to beat a table model. If you want a more detailed assessment of the different types and the numerous jobs they can be used for you will find it in 16MM FILM CUTTING and in THE TECHNIQUE OF EDITING 16MM FILMS (both published by the Focal Press). The author's name escapes me!

## SYNCHRONISERS

The other essential item you will need is that synchroniser I have already mentioned. A synchroniser has two or more large sprocket wheel locked on a common shaft which holds picture and sound in synchronism. The film is held in place by sprung rollers which can be raised to place film on the sprocket teeth and then closed to hold it in position. Once the film is locked on the sprocket teeth it will remain synchronised which ever way the sprockets turn. Some modern synchronisers have a small viewing screen built into track one so you can see a picture if one is used on that track. Magnetic sound heads, which are usually connected to an external amplifier and speaker,are often set into the other sprockets so sounds recorded on the tracks run on those sprockets can be reproduced. Most synchronisers are powered by hand. You move film through them by turning a small handle on the front or by taking up the tension on the film and winding it from one rewind to another with the synchroniser mid way between. Synchronisers are used at various stages of editing. They are ideal for synchronising rushes, and for track laying. They are also used for negative cutting but synchronisers used for that job must not have built in magnetic soundheads or it they will scratch your original.

## JOINING FILM

The other item you will need is a film joiner. When you edit a video, as I have already explained, you do not physically cut the videotape. You copy it scene by scene at pre-determined points on to another tape which becomes your edit master. When you are working on film the situation is quite different. You physically cut the film and join it together at the points where you wish your edits to be. When you are working with your cutting copy you will normally use a tape joiner. Just cut the film and your magnetic soundtracks at the points where you wish to make your edits, draw a specially thin and strong polyestre tape across the two frames on either side of your cuts and punch the sprocket holes out by lowering the handle on the joiner. Tape joins are visible on the screen. Because they cover two or more frames when the picture is projected you will see a slight variation in density when the join appears. Tape joins will also discolour with age so when the master is matched to your edited cutting copy in the last stages of editing it will not be joined with tape. The emulsion will be scraped off a small overlapping section on one side of each join and a clear adhesive known as film cement will be applied. The two pieces of film will then be brought into contact with each other and left for a few seconds so the cement can dry. A strong and invisible join will then result.

## CUTTING ROOM CONSUMABLES

When you hire a cutting room you will usually find the hire fee does not include what the company hiring the facility will describe as "consumables". You will have to buy joining tape and wax chinagraph pencils to mark your cuts. You will also need blank film to use as spacing, as we will see in a moment.

## SYNCHRONISING RUSHES

With the appropriate equipment at your command you can now start cutting. So let's look at those main stages we summarised earlier and consider in detail what they involve. The first stage - synchronising rushes - has already been summarised in an earlier chapter but what will you actually have to do to synchronise the rushes of your showreel? You can use an editing machine but you will probably find the work can be done more easily on a synchroniser. Put your reels of uncut cutting copy print and magnetic sound on the left of the synchroniser. The lab will supply your unedited film on plastic cores and not on reels. In your cutting room you should find either special reels designed to be used with those cores (split spools) or a heavy metal piece of equipment known as a "film horse" which can also be used to hold unedited film and feed it to the synchroniser. Place two empty reels on the right of the synchroniser and then open track one and put the first scene of your picture into that track. Wind it down till you find the clapper board which identifies the first scene and take on the roll. See if it is banged together. If it is not, and is simply held open, you will know that the shot is mute and will not waste time looking for sound which has never been recorded. In any event you should have camera sheets prepared by the assistant cameraman and sound sheets from the recordist to tell you what you are likely to find on each roll.

If the two parts of the board are banged together you can wind down to the first frame where the two parts of the board first touch. Mark that frame with a cross using a wax chinagraph pencil. You can then take the picture out of the synchroniser and put your un-edited sound in track two. Wind that track down till you hear an audio identification of the same scene and take. You should hear "Scene 12 Take 2 " or whatever it is followed by a bang. Make sure it is the same scene and take as the picture you have already marked. Again find the first frame of the clap where the two parts of the board have been banged together. Mark that frame - it will only be one frame - with a wax pencil cross. The sound may continue for more than one frame and in the picture the two parts of the board will remain together when they have first met but it is the first contact which produces the bang and it is thus that frame you must identify with a cross. Put both your crosses opposite each other (in level synch) in the synchroniser and wind on. Your sound and picture are now correctly synchronised.

## USING BUILD UP

You can now wind your synchronised takes on to reels on the right of the synchroniser. Run down to the point where either sound or picture cuts out. That is where your synchronism will end and you will have to re -synchronise the next shot. If the picture is longer than the sound, or if the sound lasts longer than the picture, you can build up the length by inserting blank spacing so synchronism is preserved from the head of the roll. Repeat the identification process for each shot. If you have a mute take in the middle of synchronised sound scenes you should simply build up the track by inserting spacing. If your sound runs for longer than the picture you can do the same by extending the picture with spacing until the sound cuts out. At the end of the operation you will have one reel of synchronised sound and a reel of picture which exactly matches it and your rushes will be synchronised.

You may have shot your film without any synchronised sound. Perhaps you have shot it without any sound at all and are intending to create your soundtrack in the cutting room. If that is the case you will not have any sound rushes to synchronise and can go straight on to the second stage of editing - logging your rushes.

## EDGE NUMBERS

Put your picture and any sound you have on an editing machine and run down scene by scene and take by take. On the side of the picture you will find there is a series of numbers. Those numbers were on the master film you exposed in the camera. They were invisible until the master was processed and then they became apparent. When the master was printed to make your rush print the numbers were copied too and before you cut anything at all you should make sure they are there and clearly visible. It is possible for them to be accidentally masked off when a cutting copy is printed and if that happens you will find yourself in trouble if you do not detect the problem before you start cutting. When your final edited version has been perfected those numbers will be used to match the master to your cutting copy. You can do that job yourself but I would personally suggest you leave it to a specialist technician - the negative cutter at your laboratory. Matching a master film to a cutting copy, as I have already mentioned, is known as negative cutting. It is no the most creative job in the world but it is very important. If you make a mistake and cut the master in the wrong place that mistake will be there for ever. If the master is scratched by being mishandled the damage will again be seen on every copy made from it. So, in my opinion, it is a job which is best left to people who do it all the time. To ensure they can do their job properly you must make sure that there are clear edge numbers on every reel of your cutting copy. You can do that when you log the various scenes and takes.

**LOGGING FILM RUSHES**

Note the edge numbers at the start and end of each scene and take and give a brief summary of what each shot shows. If you damage a shot while you are editing or wish to order a title or some optical effects you can then identify the master of that shot by quoting the numbers which can be traced from your log sheets in far less time than it would take to find the appropriate cans and wind through roll after roll. When your rushes have been logged you can move on to the next stage.

## SELECTING THE RIGHT SCENES AND TAKES

Your next task is to sit down and view what you have shot and determine which takes you want to use. When you shot the scenes you probably had a good idea of which takes were best but you may find when you see them afresh on a screen some shots are better than you at first thought. You will find it is worth going through everything you have shot and making a detailed list of the scenes and takes you want to include in your assembly - the first edit which is also often referred to as the "rough cut".

## BREAKING DOWN RUSHES

Your film has probably not been shot in the order in which you intend to use the various shots in your final edited version so the next job is to break down your rushes into individual shots. If the takes are long you can wind each one on a separate bobbin and hold the loose ends in place with an elastic band. If the shots are reasonably short you can hang sound and picture in a special bin known as a "cuts rack". It will have either clips or pegs at the top to hang your film from and the bin itself will probably be lined to reduce the chance of the film being scratched when it is put in and taken out. Before you hang any shots in the bin you should write the scene and take number on the head of both sound and picture with a wax pencil so it can be easily identified. That ident. serves a dual purpose. When you approach the rack you can immediately see the scene and take numbers displayed at the top and, if any strip of film should accidentally slip off the peg and fall in the bin, you will be able to identify what is when you find it.

## MAKING A FIRST ASSEMBLY

When your rushes have been broken down and all your shots are hanging in a bin or secured on separate rolls you can start to put the shots together and begin the creative part of editing. Your first task will be to get the shots in the right sequence. Cut off the slates and any sections you want to lose and pick what you feel are going to be appropriate "in" and "out" points and make them with a wax pencil. You can then either just wind the shots into one continuous roll and join them up later or you can join as you go along, scene for scene and shot for shot. At this stage you do not have to make every edit perfect. You can do that later when you make a fine cut. Experienced editors will often make a first assembly which is so good very little adjustment is required at a later date. Others editing films for the first time find it is quite enough to get the shots in the right order and approximately the right length at this stage.


## WHERE TO CUT ?

When you are cutting sound and picture on film you will find that many of the points I made about where to cut in our discussions on video editing still apply. Continuity will be a prime consideration and if you are assembling a number of shots featuring the same subject you will find that if you line up the action of the outgoing and incoming shots, as I recommended when we discussed video editing procedures, you will not go wrong. The only differences you will find are in the way you mark your cut and in the procedures you must adopt to actually make it. In video editing you enter the "in" and "out" points by pressing different keys on your edit controller. On film you mark the cutting points by physically writing on the film with a wax pencil. If you want to cut, you draw a straight line across the frame where you want the cut to be and a longer line at right angles to it, along the section you want to trim and lose. You then move to a tape joiner and cut the pictures and sounds at the points your have marked. Clean off the wax marks and draw some tape across. Bring down the handle of the joiner to press the tape home and punch holes through tape over the film's perforations. You can then project the two shots and see if the cut is what you want. Hang the trims back in the bin, again making sure they are clearly marked. When you come to make a fine cut you may wish to change one of your cutting points. If you wish to extend a shot and cannot find a trim you will be in trouble so it is worth filing all your off cuts carefully as you make each cut.

## HOW LONG FOR EACH SHOT ?

When you are making your first assembly your cutting points may be determined by a need to preserve the continuity of scripted action scenes featuring the same subject or subjects. In other situations you may feel you have almost unlimited freedom to choose where to cut. For example, you may be editing a holiday film or some other production where you have to assemble a lot of shots filmed at different locations and showing different subjects. When you are cutting two shots of the same subject together you have to watch the continuity of the action so you do not get any unwanted double takes or mismatch a movement so the action jumps. When shots have little or nothing in common the same restraints will not apply but that does not mean you should make every shot the same length.

Poorly edited films and videos are uninteresting to watch for several reasons. The most common reason is because they lack any variation in pace. You have probably seen films where shots are held for so long you find yourself praying for them to end. It is important to vary the lengths of the shots you use. How long you decide to keep each shot on the screen will to some extent depend on the subject of your film. If you are cutting a sequence in a travel film and wish to shown how peaceful life is on a selection of sun drenched beaches, you will probably want to create a relaxed atmosphere and will use shots which are held for longer than they would be if you were cutting a sequence depicting thieves being chased in a car. In the travel film you may decide to dissolve gently from shot to shot rather than emphasise the transition with a immediate cut. On the other hand, if your film does include a car chase or some other sequence where tension must be built up, skilful editing of the shots will help you to get the effect you require. By interctting shots held for a shorter duration as the chase reaches a climax you will be able to make it more exciting to watch than it will appear if you keep every shot the same length. Again must be learned in practice but by varying the length of your shots to suit the mood you want to create you will find you are able to make your film more interesting to watch.

Now you have an idea of what film editing involves we can briefly return to the opening sequence for that old cinema script we explored earlier (outline script page 143) We have seen what you would have to do to cut that sequence on video Now let's see how you would do it on film.

## CUTTING A SEQUENCE

In stead of a few neat boxes of source tapes you have about a dozen cans of film. Some contain the rush print made from the master film exposed in the camera. The others contain 16mm perforated magnetic film of sound re-recorded from your quarter inch location tapes. I am going to assume you have already used a synchroniser to synchronise sound and picture in the way we discussed just now. You have checked that the edge numbers have been printed on your cutting copy and have logged the sound and picture rushes so now you are ready to cut.

First you must break down all the takes you want to use and hang them in a bin. You can join up the takes you do not want at this stage and leave them in your rushes rolls. Just select the ones you know you want. Break them out of the rushes and write the scene and take numbers on the head of each shot. Put them in a bin or if the takes are long, keep them in separate rolls with an elastic band to hold the loose end. You can then move either to a motorised editing machine or to a synchroniser.

## USING LEADERS

On the start of your film you will need to join a leader. A leader is a length of film containing a series of numbers, usually starting at eleven or ten and running in descending order with one number to every foot of film, down to three. There are then two feet of blank film before the point at which you should join your sound or picture. Leaders serve several different purposes. They protect your cutting copy and they will enable you to lace up an editing machine or a projector without using any of the shots you want to see. They also provide an accurate count down from a clearly identifiable starting point. Film projectors do not all run up to speed instantaneously. A numbered leader will ensure that equipment is running at the right speed when your film starts. If you do not have any numbered leaders take a blank section of film and mark a start mark ( a big cross with lines round it as a box covering one frame only). It should be on a frame which is at least six feet from the start. Leave a further 8 feet of blank after the start mark and then join on your sound and picture.

## FILM FOOTAGES

You may have noticed that I said the numbers on a leader are spaced "one foot apart". Film is measured in feet. A foot of 16mm film consists of 40 frames. There are 16 frames in one foot of 35mm film and those measurements are internationally standard. We will hear more about them when we come to discuss dubbing procedures.

## STARTING TO CUT

So prepare leaders or suitable lengths of spacing with start marks on sound an picture to attach to the beginning of your first shot. If that shot is mute and there is no soundtrack for it at this stage, you will need to join blank spacing on to your leader so shots occurring later will remain in synchronisation from the start of the roll. You can now take your first shot out of the bin. It shows Tom arriving in the car park on his bicycle. It was shot with sync sound so you can run sound and picture on your editing machine and identify the point where you want to cut in. Mark it with a wax pencil and then run on to identify an out point. Mark it with a pencil on the exact frame on which you want to cut out and then move to the joiner. You can now cut and join the start of your first shot to a film leader and then wind on.

With the first shot completed you can select an in point for shot two. Again mark it and use the joiner to make your cut, laying the incoming shot opposite the cutting point you have marked as the out point of your first scene so the two pieces of film are end to end but do not overlap. Clean off the pencil marks. Pull tape across and punch the perforation holes through. You have now cut two shots together and can proceed in the same manner until the picture and background effects track of your opening sequence has been assembled.

## OVERLAYING DIALOGUE ON FILM

In that opening scene you will recall you decided to use words edited from an interview with the old projectionist as "wild" sound over shots showing him arriving for work. When those scenes were edited on tape you identified the sections you wanted to use and edited them into the second track on your edit master videotape. Working on film you can adopt a similar approach, again using a synchroniser. Find the roll containing the interview - your log sheets will help you there. Run that roll on your editing machine and mark up the sections you require. You must now compile a separate soundtrack - your new track two, which you can use to ensure the words occur at the points where you want them to be heard. To space them out and make the pauses correct you simply insert blank spacing where pauses are required. That soundtrack (your track 2) will go dead at that point but the sound effects on track one will cover you so the pauses will sound perfectly natural if you have not used too much or too little spacing and made the pauses too long or short. Join a leader on to the head of track two and run spacing down from it to the point where Tom's first words need to be heard then cut in the magnetic sound of the appropriate words. You have now edited the sound and picture of your opening scenes using two tracks and synchronising them both to your edited picture.

## OPTICAL EFFECTS ON FILM

The techniques you will have to use to produce titles and optical effects on film are also quite different to those you need to understand to produce similar effects on video. On tape the whole procedure in much simpler. By pressing a few buttons you can instantly create many of the effects you require. On film the same situation does not apply. Video is an electronic process and electronic signals can be used to instantly produce a wide range of special effects. Film is a photographic process and to make most of your effects you will need to involve a laboratory.

**A & B ROLLS**

You will recall that when a dissolve is produced one scene appears to gradually merge with another until it completely replaces it. In essence a fade out and a fade are superimposed. To get the same effect on film you must first work out where you want your dissolve to be. Run your cutting copy and select a suitable starting point, determine how many frames you wish the effect to last and then where you want it to end. You cannot physically overlap the two scenes in your cutting copy so the effect will have to be produced when your show prints are made. To do that, when your master film is neg cut it will be assembled into two separate rolls - Rolls A and B. When a dissolve or a wipe is required the assembly will move from one roll to the other so the necessary overlap can be provided at that point. The dissolves will be made by the film printing machine as the A&B roll cut master passes through. The alternative is to make a single roll optical duplicate .

**ORDERING SINGLE ROLL OPTICALS**

If you want to print your final copies from a single rolls and not incur the small additional cost of A & B roll printing, you will need to make a single roll duplicate of any dissolves and wipes you wish to include. To do that you should identify the points at which you want the effects to start and end in your cutting copy. Optical effects are usually calculated in multiples feet. You can have a one foot dissolve (over 40 frames for 16mm) which is quite short, or a longer one of 3 foot - 120 frames or almost any other combination you care to choose. To order a single roll dissolve you need to ask the laboratory to find the master of the shots you wish to dissolve from and to. Tell them where you want the effect to start and end and give them the centre point by quoting the edge numbers on the side of each shot. They will then make a single roll duplicate incorporating the dissolve you require. When working on 16mm I would personally recommend avoiding optical dupes and printing from A & B rolls when your final prints are made. The quality will be better because you will not have had to go at least one stage away from the original.

## SUPERIMPOSING TITLES ON FILM

Titles on film may also need to be superimposed in a laboratory. If your final film is only going to be shown on video you may be able to superimpose the titles electronically and make a video master from which you can produce the video copies you require. You simply wait until you have your first graded show print made from the cut master film, and then record that on a broadcast quality tape superimposing the titles electronically on the tape version in a video edit suite. That technique is used by many television companies. If you are going to need film prints for showing on a film projector you will need to know how to arrange for titles to be superimposed on film so let's see what that involves.

Again it is edge numbers which you need to refer to ensure your titles occur in the right places. You may remember that in an earlier chapter we learned how the name of a property developer appearing in an interview could be superimposed electronically during a video edit by using the "key" controls. What must you do to get the same effect on film?

First you will need to produce a title card of the lettering you require. It should be drawn using white letters on a black background. That title (often referred to at this stage as a *legend*) can then be photographed on a special black and white stock. That stock can then be processed and a high contrast print can be made from it. The shot of the background over which the title is to appear must also be cut out of its master roll and an intermediate duplicate (dupe) print must be made from it. The high contrast print and the dupe of the background are then re-exposed on a new reel of stock and a combined optical dupe, containing both the background and title is thus obtained. The lettering can be colour tinted during the last stage. The film stocks used and the exact procedure to be followed will depend on the type of film you have used in the camera to shoot your programme. Superimposing titles on film is quite a time consuming business and it is much more expensive than doping the same job on video.

So, editing a film can be more time consuming and involve more physical work than completing the various stages of post production on tape. It can also be very enjoyable and creative especially when you start to prepare a final soundtrack. In the next chapter we will see how that can be done on video and film.

# CHAPTER 7
# THE FINISHING TOUCHES

A successful freelance television producer once told me that in his opinion there were only two really enjoyable stages in the making of any film or video - signing a contract and sending out the bill ! Fortunately I realised that he was only joking for he had spent much of his life producing a range of superb programmes and clearly enjoyed every moment of his work. With your showreel now nearing completion you may be beginning to wonder if all your work is going to produce a worthwhile return. That will depend on the professionalism of your end product and on how you use it to promote your aims and in the remaining pages of this book we will explore both of those points.

## MAKING A FINE CUT

You have now been working in the cutting room for long enough to get the shots in your video in the right order and to cut them to an appropriate length. You have a programme which is beginning to take shape. You can see what the final version is going to look like but it has not yet got to a stage where you would be happy to show it to the audiences you want to impress. The production needs fine tuning. You must put those finishing touches to the work you have already done so it looks and sounds professional enough to help you to get a job.

When you have completed the first assembly of your film or video, run through it again at normal speed from start to finish and see where you feel changes need to be made. You will probably find some sequences are too long and there may be cuts which look too abrupt or which jump where they should not do so. You are also likely to find that your soundtrack is incomplete. Before you can make copies of your programme you must prepare and dubb a final soundtrack. It may need to include dialogue, sound effects, music and possibly a commentary so let us see what is involved in putting a soundtrack together. We will consider working on film first.

What audiences known as "the soundtrack" is in fact a mixture of a number of different tracks, all matching the final edited version of your picture. It will probably be easier to understand if we consider an example. Earlier in this book we looked at the opening sequence for a safety training programme (page 73) The sequence contained these shots:

1. *Two aircraft flying up and past in close formation in an air display.Their wing tips touch and they crash to the ground.*

2 *The aircraft burst into flames as they hit the ground.*

3 *A lorry parked nearby catches fire*

4 *Families who have witnessed the crash run for cover (A commentary started at this point and the action dissolved to a new location for scene 5.)*

5. *Overloaded fork lift truck drives round a corner*

6. *The driver's view - he cannot see where he is going*

7. *The truck approaches camera*

8. *Truck up and past.*

*9. A man working in the path of the truck sees it*
*approaching. Camera concentrates on the truck*

*10. The man realizes it's to late to get out of the*
*way - Zoom into his terrified face*

*11. The truck crashes.*

It was quite a simple scene. The two opening shots were filmed at an air display where things went tragically wrong and the remaining shots were staged in a factory. It took about fifteen minutes to cut the picture of that opening sequence and the editor then started to prepare his soundtracks. He used 5 different tracks to bring the scenes to life.

## LAYING SOUNDTRACKS ON FILM

He put the sound of the aircraft approaching on his first track. He used a synchroniser to lay that sound so it started level with the first frame of picture, so it could be faded in as the planes drew near. On his second soundtrack he laid the sound of the crash. It cut in on the exact frame where the planes collided. At the same point he decided to start to fade out track one, so the sound of the aircraft approaching faded out very quickly under the crash. He then used a third track to fade in the sound of the crowd's reaction. It was laid so it could be faded in as the planes crashed, thus re-creating the noises you would have heard if you had been there at the time of the crash. First the din of the planes approaching (track 1) then the unexpected crash (track 2) and the horrified screams and cries of the crowd as debris began to fall around them (track 3). The commentary then cut in on a fourth track allowing the crowd reaction to continue on track three in the background. The editor then decided to add even more detail and used a fifth track to add the sound of an ambulance approaching and passing. It was laid so it could be faded in and out under the commentary and so it could be mixed out as the location changed at the end of shot 4. An overlap was provided so the ambulance and crowd sounds (tracks 3 and 5) could be mixed across to the incoming sound of the first truck shot (track 1). That overlap meant continuing the outgoing sounds for a few seconds into the truck shot and starting the truck sound (track 1) two seconds before the shot appeared on the screen, thus allowing enough overlapped sound for a gradual transition. The remaining truck sounds were laid on the first two tracks completing a simple but quite lively opening sequence. Without those sounds the scene would have lost its drama and been much less interesting to watch.

## SOUND DUBBING

The tracks were all matched to the picture using a synchroniser. The sounds, which were all recorded on perforated magnetic film, were intercut with blank spacing so they could be laid to occur exactly where they were required. The editor then took the picture and tracks into a dubbing theatre to mix them together. The Sound Mixer who did that mixing had never seen the film before and relied on the dubbing cue sheet prepared by the editor to guide him as he worked. That cue sheet contains a lot of vital information. It specifies where each sound must start and end. The points are defined by giving footages - above each sound for the "in" points and under it for the "outs". It also told the mixer how the sounds were to be mixed. A straight line drawn across a column indicates a cut. For example, at 25 feet track two cuts in and at 39 feet track four cuts in as the commentary starts. An upturned letter "V" indicates a fade in. The figures at the top indicate where the fade must start and those at the most open point tell the mixer where the sound must reach full volume by. Track one fades in between 01 feet and 03 feet and fades out starting at 36 feet and ending by 38. When a fade out of one track and a fade in of another occurs at the same point it is known as a cross mix. Track one cross mixes to track two between 61 and 63 feet.

With well prepared tracks and cues sheets which are accurately spaced out so they are easy to follow, a satisfactory final mix can be produced without too much effort. If all the sounds were to be put on one or two tracks it would be impossible to adjust them in a creative way. Different sounds are recorded at different volume levels. If they are laid on separate tracks with enough gaps in between, the quality of each sound can be adjusted as well as its volume as the final mix is made. Voice recordings, like commentaries, should always be kept on a separate track and not intercut with sound effects.

**TRACK LAYING ON VIDEO**

Working on film, it is normal practice to prepare a number of separate tracks all recorded on perforated magnetic film but if you are editing on video you may wonder how the same results can be achieved. In fact you can follow a very similar procedure. You can lay your tracks on a multi track tape which is locked electronically to your edit master, or you build them up on a series of cassettes and then mix them together stage by stage. Your cues will be time codes and not film footages but the transitions and the overlaps you need to provide can be exactly the same as those I have suggested above.

**EDITING SOUND OFF LINE**

If you are working on video and editing off line, creating a soundtrack will not be as simple or straightforward as it will if you are editing in an on line video edit

EDITING VIDEO ON LINE

EDITING FILM WITH PICTURE AND TWO SOUND TRACKS

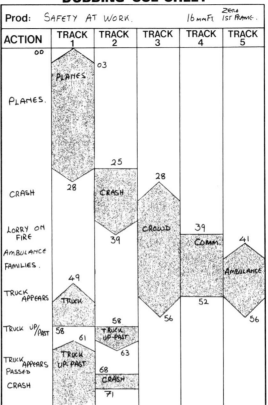
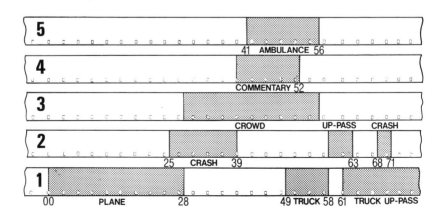

suite or cutting on film. You will be able to edit the tracks from your source recorder(s) to your offline edit master where there are likely to be two tracks available. If the equipment you are using incorporates sound mixing channels you may also be able to add sound effects and do basic sound dubbing but the quality of the final track will probably not be good enough to use on your final programme. You will have to prepare your final soundtrack on line and to do that efficiently you will need to provide very detailed notes of where you want each of your sound-tracks to start and end in your on line editing instructions.

I have already mentioned that the soundtracks of video productions are often not very impressive. One of the reasons for that is that, when people work off line, they become so obsessed with cutting the picture and synchronised dialogue tracks they tend to forget the many other sounds which may be required. When your off line is conformed on line, the soundtracks on the master tapes can be off laid to a multi track tape recorder if you provide detailed instructions on your sheets telling the on line editor where each sound can be found. You can get that information by checking each of your source tapes. When you have finalised the picture of your off line edit, run through it again and make detailed notes explaining where you want the sounds on your edited tape to start and end on the final soundtrack. You can do that by listing the time codes for the entry and exit points. You can then run through the tape again and see where those sounds need to be augmented. Make a list of the additional sounds required and the time codes at which you feel they are needed. You can then run through your source tapes and see how many of those sounds are on them. Note those time codes and you will save yourself a lot of on line editing time. Finally you can make another list of any sounds you still feel are needed but have not been able to find on your source tapes. They can be added from library dics or tapes when a final soundtrack is dubbed after the off line has been conformed.

As you can see from the paragraphs above, creating a good soundtrack is quite an involved process and it is one lazy editors and inexperienced producers are sometimes happy to overlook. They miss many creative opportunities and a lot of fun. There is considerable satisfaction in bringing scenes to life by creatively using sounds and I would urge you to make every effort to do that, whether you are working on film or video on or off line.

## CREATING VIDEO SOUNDTRACKS ON FILM

It is quite possible to produce a soundtrack for an edited video on film. I have seen a number of video productions which have been cut off line on video and dubbed using 16mm film soundtracks. In each case the editor wanted to enjoy the creative freedom of dubbing on film. They completed their picture edits off line, working on video and then arranged for the master tape to be conformed on line. Before that was done they sent the off line video cutting copy to a film laboratory and asked them to provide a 16mm film telerecorded copy of it. The quality was not memorable but you could see what was going on well enough to use it for track laying. A film editor then prepared 16mm sound-tracks to match that tele-recording and laid them, using a picture synchroniser, using the techniques we have already explored. The tracks were then dubbed in a 16mm film dubbing theatre and the final mix track was subsequently re-recorded on the master videotape after the off line had been conformed. It worked very well and, whilst it is not a procedure which is used very widely in the industry, it is another way of creating a detailed soundtrack when you are cutting off line and one you may care to bear in mind.

## VOICE OVER NARRATION ( COMMENTARY)

We have so far considered preparing sound effects tracks in some detail and have briefly mentioned commentaries but we have not yet given them the attention they deserve. Not every film or video has a commentary. Feature films and dramatised documentaries for example often use synchronised dialogue scenes rather than words spoken out of vision by a voice whose owner you never see - the basic definition of a voice over commentary. Commentaries can be a asset or a menace. You have no doubt seen many films and tapes where the commentaries have made you cringe and long to switch off and catch up with your sleep. You have probably also seen a good many where the pictures have been enhanced by words which have made them easier to follow. A good commentary will always add something to the pictures it is used with. A bad one will simply describe what you can see for yourself or tell you what you do not want to know.

## GOOD AND BAD COMMENTARY WRITING

A few days ago I saw a television documentary. It showed shots of deep sea divers descending from a yacht moored in the Caribbean to explore an old ship which had been wrecked many years ago. In the two paragraphs which follow you will find I have reproduced two commentaries. One was used on the programme which was transmitted. The second commentary was produced by another commentary writer who was asked to provide words to accompany the same shots. See which you feel is the best.

## COMMENTARY A

*Doctor Roberts has waited many years for this. As he puts on his oxygen mask, adjusts his balance and prepares to dive it must be a big moment for him. His colleagues enter the water first. It's easy to reach the wreck which has almost totally rotted away, but Dr Roberts is equipped with a bag on a rope which he intends to use to bring any treasures he finds to the surface.*

## COMMENTARY B

*The ship sank over 300 years ago with the loss of all hands. Old records suggest she may have been carrying gold. It has taken three years to find her final resting place and it will take weeks to explore the wreck properly but the water temperature here is around 25 degrees so diving is quite pleasant. If any coins are found they could be worth a fortune.*

So, which version did you prefer ? If you are in any doubt about which is good and which is not, just consider what you learned from each commentary. In version A they simply described what the action already showed. In version B each sentence made you aware of an additional point which the pictures did not explain. It made the programme more interesting to watch while version A missed many opportunities. So, if you have to write a commentary, do your research first and try to add something to the scenes the pictures present for themselves. The other mistake it pays to avoid is the error of recording "wall to wall" words. That simply means the commentary starts at the beginning of the programme and keeps going till almost the last frame. Let actions and sounds speak for themselves and act as natural punctuation marks for any additional sentences you feel are required. Commentaries are fine for introducing subjects, providing interesting facts and linking sequences together but they are a bore if they drone on for hours without making any positive contribution to what is being shown.

## WHEN AND HOW TO RECORD A COMMENTARY

Commentaries can be recorded in at least two different ways. You can record "wild" or "to picture" If you decide to opt for the first method your final commentary script can in theory be recorded at any stage of production. If you need to have the words first so you can edit pictures to them, you will need to record at an early stage, perhaps even as soon as you have viewed and logged your rushes. In most instance you are likely to find it is worth waiting until your edited picture has been finalised. The commentary may be written long before that. When you are cutting the pictures you will be able to refer to the script and read the words to yourself to ensure there are adequate pauses where the words will occur when they are recorded. Working like that will give you the freedom to make any changes which you may feel become desirable as editing progresses. Practice suggests that you may find words or possibly sentences and paragraphs which need to be adjusted to suit pictures which work better when they are assembled in a way which was not originally envisaged. I can think of numerous occasions when that has occurred. By delaying your commentary recording until the picture has been finalised you can give yourself the freedom to make whatever adjustments are needed without paying for the commentary to be recorded twice.

## RECORDING WILD AND TO PICTURE

With a final script and fine cut picture you can still record your commentary in one of two ways. You can run through script before a recording session is arranged and put the time codes ( or if you are cutting on film the footages), opposite the start of each paragraph. When you come to record, you can run the picture on one machine and a blank tape or reel of film on another with the two locked in synchronisation. The time code or footage can be projected on a counter under the screen or superimposed on it and you can then cue your narrator to speak at the points where each paragraph is due to begin. You will usually find if you actually press the cue light button about a second (or one film foot) before the point where the words are actually required the narrator will react and start to speak at precisely the right point. This techniques is known as "recording to picture". It can work very well if your commentary is properly written and cued and if there are not too many words. If there are, you can probably identify the problem and correct it when you run through with a script before you make a final recording.

The second way of recording a commentary is to record it "wild". That, as you have no doubt already worked out, means recording without projecting the picture. Your narrator still sits in a sound proof commentary booth but on this occasion he or she cannot see the picture. It may not have been edited and is thus not ready for showing. You do not have any time codes or footage cues and simply record what is written in the script on a blank roll of tape or film. You can then return to the cutting room and edit it to match the picture.

When recording wild, always bear in mind the scenes you are intending to use the words you are recording with. Are the words going to be to long for the shots you intend to use to illustrate them ? Is the narrator pausing at the points where you are going to  make your edits or is the inflection going to be wrong when you insert a pause ? Considering points like that before you record can save a lot of problems in the cutting room.

## MANAGING A RECORDING SESSION

When a commentary is recorded the narrator, or narrators if you are using more than one voice, will need to be in a sound proofed room so you only hear their voices and not other background sounds. You will have to hire a suitable sound studio. You can hire such facilities for an hourly rate which will include all the equipment you need and the services of a Sound Recordist. You simply have to provide any picture you want to record to, and the narrator you intend to use. Narrators will expect to be paid a fee based on the duration of the film or video and the type of use it is intended for.
 A relatively unknown name will normally charge you about the same as a good meal for four in a smart hotel to record a 10 minute commentary for a documentary intended for educational house use. If you are recording for a world-wide tv series the charge will be much higher and in any case you will need to negotiate before any recording dates are fixed.

## CONTRACTING THE RIGHT ARTISTES

Voice over artistes need special skills. Everyone thinks he or she could read a commentary but in practice even experienced actors are not always able to do it satisfactorily. Bringing meaning to words which are often dull without appearing in vision requires special abilities and a quality of voice which will stand out well when it is dubbed over music and sound effects. There are agencies which specialize in providing artistes for voice over work and you may be able to contact artistes who you have noticed doing a good job on other people's productions. Choose the right voice for the job. A formal newsreader may be quite wrong for a relaxed holiday film.

He has been trained to speak without emotion and to give facts in an unbiased manner. A voice which is perfect for reporting the nation's nightly news may make a less formal subject sound dated and un appealing. Ask to hear demonstration tapes and pick the right voice or voices for the production you are making.

## ADDING MUSIC

Another element you may feel you wish to include in your soundtrack is some music. You may decide you want to have music specially composed or you may decide to opt for one of the thousands of pre-recorded "mood" music discs which are available and which are internationally clearable. If you want music specially composed for your production, you will need to provide your composer with a time coded copy of your final edited picture. He or she will then use that as a guide and compose the music you need. It will be pre-recorded on tape to fit the time coded sections where you have indicated music is required in your edited cutting copy. You can then arrange for it to be transferred to film or video and lay it alongside your other tracks ready to dubb.

## CUTTING TO MUSIC

If you decide to use music which has already been recorded for general film and video use, you can go about it in two different ways. First you can select the pieces you wish to use by listening to disks or tapes. That music will then need to be re-recorded either on film or on a tape which can be synchronised to your video. If you want to "lay" it, making it fit pictures you have already cut, you can follow the procedures we have already discussed. Insert the music tracks where they are needed and cue them on your dubbing cue sheet. The alternative way of using music is to edit your pictures to match the beat of the music scene for scene and cut for cut. Cutting to music can be very effective providing it is not overdone. If every music sequence is obviously cut to match the tempo of the music, audiences may become wary of the technique but it can work well if it is not used too much.

To cut a sequence to music on video you must first lay the music down on one of the tracks on your video edit master. Select the track you intend to use on your edit controller and then replay the master disk or tape and simultaneously re-record it on your master tape. If you have already cut sequences on either side of the points at which you want your music sequence to occur you may find it difficult to start and finish at a precise enough point when you are replaying from a tape or disk. If that situation occurs it is quite acceptable to transfer the tape or disk to another broadcast quality tape and then edit that transfer into your master tape. Any small loss of quality is unlikely to be noticed providing you check your recording levels before you re-record on each occasion. You can then return to the edit controller and indicate that you no longer wish to record on the track which you have put your music on but in stead wish to edit the picture. Press V for a video edit and then cut your pictures to match the tempo and beat of the music on your track. If you are working on film you simply re-record the music you want to use on perforated magnetic film. Run it on an editing machine and mark the back of the magnetic track with a chinagraph pencil at the points where you want your edits to occur. You can then use either a picture synchroniser or a motorised editing machine to insert pictures at each point.

**FOREIGN LANGUAGE VERSIONS**

If your film or video is intended for international showing you may need to produce different language versions. A major international feature film will need to be completely re-voiced with the parts spoken in vision being spoken again by actors in the language required for each country and synchronised so the new words fit the original lip movements. That technique, which is known as post synchronisation, is one you are unlikely to be involved in making your showreel. You may however wish to translate and dubb a voice over commentary or explain what people appearing in synchronised interviews shown in vision are saying to audiences who do not understand the original language.

## M & E TRACKS

If you know you may have to prepare different language versions, when you mix your soundtracks together you should make a pre - mix before you complete your final mix master. A pre - mix should include all your music and sound effects tracks and any dialogue spoken by people appearing in vision. It should not include any voice over commentary. Pre-mixes are also known as *M & E tracks* The letters stand for music and effects. International Sound Band is another term which you may come across in some European countries.

## DUBBING COMMENTARIES IN OTHER LANGUAGES

If you have an M & E track you can produce a foreign language version of a straightforward documentary with relatively little effort. If the film or video soundtrack just consists of music, sound effects and a voice over commentary the first step to take is to get the commentary translated into the language you wish to use. Be careful when you arrange for a translation to be done. Translating commentaries has almost as many pitfalls as writing them in the first place. The first point to bear in mind is that the translated text must be about the same overall length as the original or else it will not fit the slot available. Some languages are rather long winded and it can be difficult fitting them into gaps originally filled by an English commentary. Arabic is particularly difficult and Chinese and Tagalog have given me plenty of headaches. It is also important to ensure that whoever you entrust with translating your script is used to writing words which are intended to be spoken and not read in a brochure. If you give a script to a brochure writer to translate the result may not flow when it is read aloud. The narrator who is going to read the translated script may well be the best person to undertake the translation but always get it checked by a third party who speaks the language concerned before you record. When you give your translator the original script try to also give him or her a video copy of the original language version so the meaning of each sentence cannot be misunderstood, then you should manage to avoid problems later.

**DUBBING OVER INTERVIEWS**

If your film or video includes synchronised sound interviews, when you prepare other language versions, if you do not wish or cannot afford to re-voice the people appearing in the pictures, you will find it is normally acceptable to hear the original language for a few seconds and then fade it down and superimpose another voice in the new language, reading what is being said. You will need to establish the original voice first and let audiences see who is speaking so the translation does not sound like bad re-voicing. As that pause will make the available space fractionally shorter, the time loss will also need to be borne in mind when the translation is done.

When you have a script and narrators who speak the languages you wish to record, you can return to a recording studio and, using the footage or time code cues you used for the original version, record the new commentary and then edit it to fit. If the subject of your video is one of international interest you may find you are able to make substantial international sales with good foreign dubbing.

## MAKING COPIES OF YOUR FINAL EDITED VERSION

Your first production is now nearing completion. Soon you will be able to put it to work. You have now edited a final version, recorded any commentary and dubbed a final soundtrack. One stage remains. You must make copies of the final version in the formats you require.

If you have been working on film up to this stage, for the last stages of your production you will again need the help of your film laboratory. By the time you have finished dubbing you will have an edited cutting copy and a master final mix magnetic soundtrack. If you have been shooting and editing on 16mm film they are like to be on 16mm stock if you have been shooting on 35mm it is probably they will both be on 35mm stock but that does not mean your final copies will always have to be in those formats. Likewise if you have shot and edited on Betacam SP or some other form of videotape it does not mean that your programme can only be made available on the same type of cassettes. All the different film and video formats can be interchanged and if you know what to do you can make copies of almost anything for showing anywhere in the world, so let's' see how you can go about it.

## PRODUCING VIDEO COPIES

If you have worked throughout on video your edit master will be a cassette which is either PAL, NTSC or SECAM. The moment you have completed a master tape which you are entirely happy with, arrange for it to be copied on the same format for safety purposes. Keep that duplicate tape in a different place to the edit master, then if an accident occurs, you will not have lost all the work you have put into editing and dubbing. It is always worth making a safety copy. I recall one producer who never bothered and told everyone he looked after his master tapes as if they were his children and nothing could possibly ever happen to them. Unfortunately it did. One cold winter night a water pipe on the floor above his cutting room froze up and burst flooding everything below. Many master tapes were lost and that particular producer now offers different advice.

## VIDEO COPIES IN DIFFERENT FORMATS

With your master and a safety copy at your disposal you can now start to prepare copies in any other formats you require. If you are proposing to sell your production for television showing another broadcast cassette will be required. If you have shot on PAL and wish to sell to America or France or any of the other countries which do not have a PAL television system as standard, ( There is a full guide on pages 32 and 33) your master or safety tape will need to be converted when copies are produced. There will be a slight loss of quality but if the original is good it will not cause you or your customers any concern.

For general showing you will probably require copies on VHS and in the USA perhaps also on Betamax. Again they can be produced by replaying either your master or the duplicate and re-recording on the type of cassette required. If you are changing standards between PAL/ NTSC or SECAM a signals converter will again be required. Copies of any cassette can also be made on Hi 8 or video 8 and the quality should be fine for general showing. I often keep a selection of the programmes I have produced on 8mm cassettes in my briefcase. I also carry a video Walkman so if someone wants to see a particular production in a street in a car or on a plane, I can slot in a cassette and the show can begin. You may find that is a useful way of promoting your talents and services.

## FILM COPIES OF VIDEOS

Videos can also be copied on to film. Until quite recently that is a course I would not have recommended for anything except dubbing but recent developments in film stocks and in the equipment available to make film copies have made it possible to produce quite acceptable results. The work must be done by a film laboratory and you should select the lab you use for its experience of this specialist type of work. Not every lab will do it. If you find one which says it can help ask to see examples of what they have produced in the past from master tapes of the same format as yours before you commission what is likely to be quite an expensive process.

I recently produced a tourist video for a customer who originally said he was only going to want the production for showing on video in five European countries. It was shot on Betacam SP, following all the processes we have explored in this book. When it was completed it was very well received and the customer decided he wanted to arrange for a copy to be shown at a prestige gathering in one on London's largest cinemas. I told him I thought that was a very bad idea and tried to dissuade him from following that course but he would not be swayed. I approached a number of laboratories and eventually found one which I knew had a superb reputation for quality and asked them to undertake a test. The lab took my edit master tape and tele-recorded it on Eastmancolor negative film. They graded the negative and made a print which they invited me to view. I arrived armed with dark glasses and aspirins expecting to see the worst and was amazed by the quality of the print they showed. The colours were good and the image was still agreeably sharp. That copy was subsequently shown on a large cinema screen and the results were quite acceptable, so it can be done !

## SOUND FOR FILM COPIES OF VIDEOS

If you decide to make 16mm or 35mm films copies of a video you must ensure that your original tape is pin sharp and of optimum quality. You will also need to identify one frame of your soundtrack before the video starts so, when the magnetic sound on your master tape is re -recorded as a photographic optical track for printing alongside the picture, that frame can be identified and the new sound and picture negatives can be synchronised. The best way to do that is to cut one frame of thousand cycle tone into your track at the end of the VTR clock. You will understand the reasons for doing that more clearly if you study the section on magnetic and optical sound which you will find below.

## FILM AND VIDEO COPIES OF PRODUCTIONS SHOT ON FILM

If your production has been shot on film you can show it in any film or video format. If you have shot on 16mm, your master film will be neg cut and printed on to a reel of un-joined 16mm positive stock to make your first show print. That print can be shown on any 16mm projector. It can also be recorded on video by lacing it on a telecine projector and simultaneously recording the output of that machine on video reels or cassettes. If you are proposing to make video copies you will find it pays to ask your lab to print your cut master on a special low contrast telecine print stock. The colour of your video copies will look better and the definition will be sharper.

16mm films can be enlarged to 35mm by making a 35m inter-negative from the 16mm original. 16mm copies of 35mm productions can be made by reversing the process and printing a cut 35mm neg on to 16mm stock or by making a duplicate 16mm inter-negative if a lot of copies are required. Your laboratory will be able to give you advice on the best way of producing the copies you require.

## MAGNETIC AND OPTICAL SOUND

The sound on video copies can be recorded directly from your master video tape or from a 16mm or 35mm magnetic final mix master if you have been working on film. If you want film copies you will have to choose the type of soundtrack you require on the copies you produce. There are two types of film soundtrack  - magnetic and optical. While you were editing you will have worked with separate magnetic tracks. The picture you have cut will be mute like the original film exposed in the camera and your final soundtrack will also be on a separate magnetic film.  If you are going to show your finished film on television or record it on video, a telecine projector will be able to run the mute show print of your picture in synchronisation with your final mix master magnetic soundtrack but if you want film copies for showing on conventional 16mm projectors you are more like to require copies which have a combined optical soundtrack.

An optical track, as you may already know, looks like a wavy line down the side of the picture. It is printed by a photographic process and you will need a sound negative before you can make combined optical (abbreviated as *comopt*) copies for general showing. To make that, replace the number three on the leader of your final mix master magnetic film soundtrack with one frame of thousand cycle tone. You can then send that track off to the laboratory and ask them to re-record it as an optical sound negative. Tell them what sort of picture master you need are going to ask them to print it with so they produce a track with the right geometry.

When the new sound neg is processed you will immediately see why it was worth inserting that frame of thousand cycle tone. The negative will look like a series of wavy lines. It will be hard to identify any specific point. When you were working with magnetic tracks there was always a numbered leader to tell you where the start was and to use when synchronising the picture and other tracks but there is no leader on your new optical sound negative so how can you synchronise it to the newly cut picture master ? You can do it by locating that frame of tone you cut into the mag track leader. It will stand out as one frame of closely spaced lines and it will occur before the rest of the programme starts. You can recall where you put that frame of tone on your mag leader - replacing the figure three. Now put that wavy frame of tone on your new sound negative opposite the figure three on the leader of your edited picture master and your sound and picture will again be in level synchronisation, as they were when you edited

## SOUND ADVANCE FOR COMOPT FILM COPIES

There is one more move you must make before you can produce comopt film copies of your final edited film. The sound on combined optical prints is not level with the picture. In editing you always cut in level synch - with sound and picture exactly opposite each other but if you think of the layout of a conventional film projector you will quickly realize that the same situation does not apply. The optical sound gate is ahead of the picture gate so the soundtrack must be advanced by that amount when comopt prints are made. For 16mm copies the sound will need to be advanced by 26 frames ( so it is 26 frames ahead of the picture) and for 35mm comopt prints it must be advanced by 20 frames.

Now you have edited your showreel and know how to make the copies you require. In the next and last chapter we will see how you can put your talents to work and start to make some money.

# CHAPTER 8
# SELLING YOURSELF

Making your showreel you will have learned a great deal and will probably now realize how much more there is to learn to reach a high professional standard. Don't let that worry you. One of the nicest things about working in film and television is that there is always something new to learn or a new way to do a job you have done many times before. When you are starting your career the important thing is to learn as much as possible before you try to promote yourself and to recognize that you don't know it all and there is still plenty to learn. Your showreel will help you to get a job or set up your own business - unless it is a disaster and clearly demonstrates a complete lack of talent.

## ASSESSING YOUR OWN WORK

When work on your showreel has been completed sit down and view it for the first time right through without a stop in whatever format you are intending to show it in. How does it look ? Are the pictures sharp and the colours accurate ? How does it sound ? Have you used both sound and picture as creatively as possible or does your track sound like an afterthought ? Does the programme flow along in an interesting way without any embarrassing pauses or sequences which seem too long ? You will find it is quite difficult to assess these points because you will be too close to the subject. You have been involved from the initial concept. Audiences will only be involved for as long as your programme takes to show and their views will be conclusive. They will or they will not, like what you have done .

## A PROFESSIONAL APPRAISAL

If you know someone who is already employed in a responsible position in the industry, you may care to ask them to look at your production before you start to show it to a wider and more important audience. A second opinion from a well qualified person can be helpful. Do not expect to be showered with praise. If you have done a good job you will no doubt be commended but any worthwhile review may include criticism. You will probably be told what the reviewer thinks is wrong and may be given constructive suggestions which may help you with your next film or video. Don't expect a written report. If the person you have approached is any good, he or she will probably be busy and may not have time to put anything on paper but you may be able to discuss the points which have been raised and find you learn even more as a result of that discussion.

## APPLYING FOR A JOB

Now you can start to promote your talents. You may wish to get a job with a film or tv company or to set up your own business. In this chapter we will see what you are likely to encounter. First we will consider applying for a job with an established company

*Dear....*

*Thank you for your letter asking if we have any jobs in this company. We have studied your application and regret that we do not have any suitable vacancies at this time. We will however keep your letter of file and notify you should a suitable vacancy occur.*

*Yours....*

If you have already tried writing letters applying for jobs you may have received a letter like the one I have reproduced above. Alternatively you may not have received any reply at all. So how can you avoid such a blunt dismissal ? As always in life, it pays to consider other peoples points of view.

For many years I answered every job application letter I received personally. Today I am afraid I find it is impossible to do that any longer because I receive far too many. They fall into three different categories. There are those which are obviously being sent to every company the writer has been able to find by studying various directories. Then there are those where the writer has picked a few names at random and sent a printed sheet with an accompanying letter beginning "Dear Sir or Madam". I also receive some which are personally addressed and written by people who are clearly interested in the sort of business we are in and have gone to great lengths to learn something about it. I still try to answer them but, as we have had only a handful of staff changes over thirty years, have hardly ever been able to offer anyone a job. What I can do is tell you what you should say in a preliminary letter and what you should avoid saying at all costs.

When you are trying to sell a product or service to a customer, who initially probably does not want to know anything about it, you need to present what you are selling to your potential customer in the way which is most likely to appeal to him or her. You must be honest. It is quite useless claiming you have experience and qualifications you have never possessed. Even if you were able to land a job in that way, your lack of experience would soon be discovered. Try to put yourself in the position of the person you are writing to. What have you got to offer that he might be interested in ? If you have a showreel that could be a door opener. You could offer to show it and ask if a few minutes could be found to give you some advice. That can open doors - sometimes wide enough for you to get a foot inside on a more permanent basis. When you write a letter always try to make sure it is personally addressed to whoever you want to see. If there is a Personnel Manager that may be the right person to contact. In a smaller company it may be the President or the Managing Director. In my view it is a mistake to simply address a letter with a job title. If you are interested in that company and are hoping they may employ you should find out the name of the correct person to approach and address you letter accordingly. That at least shows you have been interested enough to do some research. If you get an interview you will find it is very much in your interests to discover all you can about the organisation you are going to see. What sort of programmes do they make ? Have you seen anything they have done? What do you know about them? If you want to join them they are likely to be more impressed if they find you have taken the trouble to find out what they are involved in and not simply picked their name out of a directory.

So, when writing a preliminary letter these are the key points it helps to remember.

1) *Do some research.* Don't just pick names out of a directory. Find out what sort of work they are involved in

2) *Address letters personally* and make sure you get the spelling right ! People are not impressed by letters which are obviously intended to be personal but in practice are not. I recently received a letter from a well known credit card company. It began "Dear Mr Binder. This letter is personal to you". That was followed by three paragraphs of guff trying to persuade me to have a card I have already possessed for several years. Under the signature of a Vice President, there was an additional paragraph which read: "P.S. If this offer does not interest you please pass the information on to a friend"! You will not be

surprised to learn that letter ended up in a bin. If your job application is not to take the same route you will need to avoid the mistakes that letter contained.

3) *Produce tangible evidence* of your interest in the sort of work you are applying to do. Saying you are interested in film and tv is fine but proving you have enough interest to be worth employing is a very different matter. If you want to make films and videos it is no use saying you have been working in insurance for five years or have sold goods in a shop. If that is all the experience your can produce you might just as well leave your letter unwritten. It is quite acceptable to have done a different kind of job but you must be able to show that you have also done all you can to foster a genuine ambition to make films or videos. That may have involved doing one job during the day and studying at night. You are very unlikely to stand any chance of being short-listed unless you can show that you have made every effort to prove your interest in doing the sort of work you are now asking to be paid to do.

If you have a showreel you can offer to send that or ask if they would be kind enough to spare a few moments and give you their comments. That may not immediately get you a job but if the showreel is good and they happen to be considering taking on someone new, it could tip the balance in your favour. At least it will show that you have done everything you can to learn and follow up your interest.

4) *Supply a CV* ( Curriculum Vitae) It is not essential to supply this but if you have qualifications and experience which you think will help you it may be worth including a CV with a first or with a follow up letter. CVs's need to look neat and to be clearly laid out. Dates are important. Employers want if you are capable of retaining a job for a worthwhile period. Your school record

could help if you have not changed schools every 3 months and failed everything in sight. List the schools you attended and any qualifications you got. That will show a potential employer that you have an ability to learn and have acquired enough knowledge to get some paper qualifications. If you have attended a University or college give details of that and list any jobs you have held since then with the dates concerned. Don't worry if your first job was not a particularly good one. No one expects you to start at the top. What they will want to know is how long you held your job or jobs for, so they can see if you are likely to be worth employing or if you are going to prove to be a liability. As well as providing details of your qualifications and experience you should give at least three references. They should be employers, school staff or people in responsible positions who have known you for some time. Ask the people you are proposing to mention if they are happy to let you include their names on your list and then they will be prepared if someone contacts them.

## FOLLOWING UP YOUR APPLICATION

When you send off a job application don't expect to receive a reply overnight. You no doubt feel your letter is very important but the recipient will have many more pressing matters to deal with. If you have not had a reply after three or four weeks you may care to write again or even ring up to check that your initial letter was received. I am afraid you will find you get a lot of rebuffs. There is no easy way of getting your first job and you will need to be very persistent. I do not mean that when someone says "no" you have to go on at them trying to persuade them to change their minds. If they say there are no vacancies you must assume that is correct and will probably be wasting your time trying to persuade whoever has told you that to change their minds. You will however need to persist in trying every possible avenue until you find a door which opens. It will be extremely discouraging. You may begin to wonder if it is worth trying any more but do not let discouragement get the better of you. Look at the people in the industry today - There are thousands of them working all over the world and they all had to start somewhere. Many if not most will have faced the same discouragements when they first started out. If your showreel is good in due course it will help you to find the right opening.

## WORKING WITH OTHERS

There is one qualification I have not mentioned in my comments on introductory letters though I did briefly mention it earlier. It is probably the most important qualification of all. It's the ability to get on with other people. To listen and learn and appreciate other points of view. Without that ability you are unlikely to get anywhere. Paper qualifications like degrees and examination passes show you have a brain and an ability to assimilate knowledge but if you have an abrasive personality you are unlikely to get far. You will do better if you are a good film maker, without any paper qualifications but with the ability to talk to people and get on with them in a any situation.

## JOB INTERVIEWS

If you apply for an advertised job or as a result of writing your application letters, you will eventually be invited to attend an interview. You will notice I have said *will be* invited. Not *may* be invited, or could be. I have chosen that word quite deliberately. After making numerous job applications and getting nowhere you may feel it is all hopeless but if you are any good you will eventually get where you want to go. Being invited to attend an interview will be the first step on your ladder to success. What is likely to happen then and how should you approach a preliminary interview?

You may be asked to attend an informal meeting or a formal appointments board type interview like the BBC situation I described in chapter one. That was my first experience of any job interview and I was terrified at the prospect. " Make sure you wear dark socks", one friend had advised me. "If you wear a bright colour they will think you are too trendy". I took his advice. Then I would have taken advice from anyone ! The interview passed quite painlessly.

If you are attending any interview you will find it pays to look smart. You don't have to go out and buy the latest suit or over-dress by wearing the sort of clothes you would not normally wear, but you should make every effort to look clean and tidy. You must look as if you are worth investing in, and if you look as if you cannot be bothered to look after yourself, why should you expect any employer to put money on you. It is a good idea to get a good night's sleep before any important interview. You will find it is easier to deal with any difficult questions if your mind is alert. Always be completely honest. If you lie when you give your answers you will soon be found out and those interviewing you may well be experienced enough to detect that the answers you are providing are not the truth. If you are nervous don't let that put you off. It is perfectly natural and the people you are going to see will understand. It will not put them off and they will probably do all they can to put at ease. You should avoid trying to fortify yourself with alcohol. A few drinks beforehand may make it seem easier at the time but that is an illusion. The booze may calm you down but it will also affect your judgement and slow down your response time. If you smell like a brewery or sound slurred it will not help you. Drugs of any kind should be avoided too. I can recall at least one career which ended before it could begin because a young applicant got that one wrong. He had reached the last ten on a short-list of candidates for a job as a television cameraman. He had supplied a videotape which was quite impressive. I personally had a high opinion of that particular candidate, based largely on the video he had sent with his application. His CV was short but he was young. He had worked in several pubs over a period of months to get enough money to take a course on professional film making. That course had clearly taught him a lot. For someone who had only been on one course and had made his own way without any outside financial help, his efforts were impressive and I looked forward to meeting him when he came before the Appointments Committee. Alas, when he arrived he was hopelessly drunk. The interview was terminated almost before it could begin and he was not offered the job.

## ASSESSING THE SUCCESS OF YOUR SHOWREEL

The showreel you have produced will act as a show-case for your talents. In time, if you have done a good job, in due course it should help you to get a job with an established company or it may encourage someone to commission you to make a video or film for them. If that showreel is your first production it will always be special, not because it will be the best programme you will ever make but because you will have had more fun and learned more making it that you will on any future occasion. You may have learned so much that you already feel it is awful and not want to show it! If that is the case your efforts have still not ben wasted if have learned enough to recognize what is wrong. You may be able to amend any errors which you can now identify or correct shortcomings which others have drawn to your notice.

Do not spend too much time changing your first production. If you set yourself high standards you will probably never be entirely satisfied with your first production and you could spend the rest of your life making alterations and never do anything else. Unless it is a complete disaster it will do a useful job for you. If you want to be a cameraman and have shot the showreel yourself it will show that you have a good idea of how to frame and light pictures and know what basic camera movements are all about. If you aim to be an editor it will show that you have learned the basic editing techniques and do not hold shots too long or cut them at the wrong points. If sound is your principal interest, anyone listening to your showreel will be able to appreciate that you have used the right microphones at each location and have positioned them in the right place to record sounds which are not distorted or difficult to hear. So, one way or another - even if a potential employer only sees a few minutes of the programme you have slaved for months to complete -, it is likely to prove worthwhile. If you have done a really good job it could launch you on a great career. You may even be in a position to sell your own expertise as an independent film or video producer working as a self - employed person or setting up your own business. Again you may care to know what is likely to be involved.

## TAKING A COMMERCIAL VIEW

You may want to make films or videos professionally because you enjoy doing it. If you are going to make enough money to live on, you will also need to keep a close check on the business side of things. We can all go out and make videos about the subjects we enjoy, and go bankrupt in the process. Making movies professionally is like any other business. It's very competitive and essential to minimise costs and produce enough profit to live on and to invest in the future. To do that you must have a viable product or service to offer and you must know how to bring it to the attention of potential customers.

## YOUR OWN BUSINESS ?

If your showreel is a success and you do not want to become a full time employee working for a tv network or an independent company, you can always try to set up in business by yourself or in partnership with someone you trust. You should be aware that customers will not be beating a path to your door the moment you decide to set up. You will be faced with thousands of competitors, many of whom will already have some very useful contacts. If your showreel has been well received and you feel you know enough to try establishing your own venture you may find it is worth giving it a try. You do not have to have enormous resources though if you have it will undoubtedly help. When I left the BBC after a number of years, I decided to start an independent company. We had vast capital - I think it was around £10.00! Our other assets were also unlikely to attract an immediate takeover. We had a clockwork Bolex camera which was twenty years old and a projector which has been used during the war. With those assets alone we would not have got far but we also had quite a lot of experience of professional television production and some ideas which we thought might work. That was over thirty years ago and over those years we have been fortunate enough to produce programmes which have been used in 27 countries. So, anyone can do it if you have enough experience to convince potential customers that you know what you are doing and if the results you produce are good enough to encourage others to give you work.

## STARTING A BUSINESS

If you decide you want to run your own business your must first decide what type of business you want to run and then choose whether you want to set up on your own or to go into business with a friend or colleague. You can trade as a limited company or a partnership or simply register yourself as a business name. Limited companies are supposed to be safer because if things go wrong creditors can only seize the assets of the company. Its liabilities are limited as the title suggests. In a partnership or as a sole trader, if things go wrong in theory and often in practice creditors can claim all your assets - not just those involved in running the business. They can claim your house and any other valuable possessions you may have to repay your debts. To reach the correct decision you will need professional advice from people who are qualified to point you in the right direction. At the start and throughout your business life you will need a good solicitor and an accountant.

A solicitor will be able to give you advice on the difference between the different types of business, along the lines which I have briefly mentioned above. He will know much more about the legal position than I do and he will be able to give you enough facts to help you to make a decision. An accountant will advise you on the tax implications of working from rented or purchased premises or even from home. You will need his help with many other financial matters as the business grows. Choose your advisers carefully. Large firms of accountants and solicitors often have very high overheads. They would no doubt love to take your money but if they are used to dealing with international groups they may not be that interested in the activities of a small new concern with very few assets. Perhaps you have a friend who is already in business who can point you in the right direction.

**CHOOSING A PARTNER**

You may wish to start a business with a friend or perhaps someone who has been involved in making your showreel. You can do that by either establishing a partnership in which you are both equally involved or by both becoming Directors of a company which is jointly owned. I realize that you want to make films and videos and are probably not that concerned about following all the correct procedures which should be considered when setting up a business but please don't ignore them. Before you do any business at all you should draw up a plan and either a contract or a letter or agreement which should be signed by all the people who will jointly own and run the business. Your solicitor will help you. You should agree with whoever is going to be your associate or partner the basis on which the business will be run. In simple terms that means saying who is going to do what, who the shareholders are and how any profits are going to be divided. You can own the company jointly with a nominal share capital. If there aren't any assets all this formality may seem a waste of time but if you do not get the basic facts in writing at the outset, in years to come you may regret it.

I had lunch recently with a Producer who has been in the business about as long as I have. He has made some wonderful films and is a man whose talents I have always admired. I had not seen him for some months and when we met for lunch his appearance gave me a shock. He has always been busy with a long list of commissions for projects of every kind. He made a lot of money and, as I discovered at that lunch, lost most of it because he failed to get the documentation right when he started his company .

He formed a partnership with a colleague. They were both young and they got on well. As the business grew they both got married and their wives took an interest in the company which grew and prospered. They moved to larger premises and did very well until, without any warning, one of the wives walked out on her husband and sued him for divorce. It was a shattering blow but worse was to come. After a very expensive court settlement in which she claimed her husband owned much more than he did, she departed. As he was unable to dis -prove her words because no business agreement had ever been put in writing, he had to pay up. The strain on the business began to show and customers went elsewhere. In six months both men lost almost everything they and suddenly found they had wasted the best years of their lives. So, make sure that cannot happen to you and get professional advice from day one.

**RENTING BUSINESS PREMISES**

If you decide to start your own business you will need to decide where you are going to work from. You could start at home but you may find it is better to rent an office. If you work from home, you may have to pay a commercial business tax for the portion of the house you use for your work. You may also find that if you decide to sell the property you will charged a profits tax on the same area. You can hire an office on a short lease or even by the hour. When we first started we hired office space one day a week and tried to see any customers who wanted to see us on that day ! It saved us money but it was difficult to work. Fortunately the business grew quickly enough for us to take a long lease and then to buy our own building and hopefully you will find the same. The important point is not spend more than you can afford. Plush offices are all very nice but they are not going to increase your income. In some businesses people may be impressed by smart premises and flashy cars. In film and television there are some who feel that is still the case and I did once, but I have since discovered that if potential customers like what they see on a screen they don't care if you are working from the north pole. If they like what you are doing they will still come to you.

## CHECKING A LEASE

If you decide to rent a building get your solicitor to check the lease before you sign. Watch for any renewal clauses. If you have been offered a short lease with a renewal every two or three years, the landlords will probably be entitled to increase the rent at each renewal. That is one of several points it pays to look into before you sign. You should also ensure that the obligations of landlords and tenants are clearly defined. Are you responsible for internal and/or external repairs? If the landlord is responsible for outside maintenance it could save you a fortunate. You do not want to suddenly be told you have got to pay for a new roof. Access routes can also give you problems. If you feel you may need to work late, make sure there is 24 hour access or you may find you are locked out of your own offices at half past five. In film and television hours tend to be long and a normal office lease may have unacceptable restrictions. Finally, establish how the rent is to be paid. Is it once a year or quarterly and does it need to be paid in advance ? They are all simple points but if you get them wrong and have signed a lease without checking, it may cost you money you do not want to pay.

## ACQUIRING EQUIPMENT

To produce the films or videos which you hope are going to make your money you will also need quite a lot of film or video equipment. If you do not have the money to buy it outright there are several other ways of acquiring what you need. You can buy on hire purchase or arrange to lease. Alternatively you can hire any specific items you need for the days on which they are required. It is common practice to hire cameras for a shoot and, as I have already explained, cutting facilities can be hired on a weekly basis. You may eventually probably wish to buy your own equipment or establish your own editing facilities but in the interim you may be wise not to tie up large sums of cash on items which are not going to be in continuous use. Deciding when to buy, or indeed if it is worth buying at all, is not as straightforward as it may at first sound. Again it is worth talking to your Accountant. In theory, when there is enough work to keep you busy, it makes sense to buy what you need and to write that cost off over a period of three to five years.

**BUY, HIRE OR LEASE ?**

In practice, when it comes to buying cameras, technology is changing so fast it may be wiser to hire or lease unless you have scenes to be shot almost every day, when buying will always be the favourite option. If you lease you may find there are tax advantages. You can also use hire purchase which will again give you all the items you need earlier than you would be able to afford them if you were to buy them outright. When you own little or no equipment it is very tempting to buy everything on HP but watch out for high interest charges. It is so easy to enter into an agreement when business is good and then hit a flat period and find your resources are severely stretched. Before you enter into any lease or HP contract remember to add up the other costs you are going to have to meet on a regular basis while you are making the repayments. Rent, taxes, telephones, electricity, wages and possibly other costs will have to be met every month. You will find the figures soon add up. If you have six bad months with no new orders, will the HP deal you are considering still seem such a good proposition ? That is a question you should ask yourself before you sign up.

## EQUIPPING YOUR OFFICE

You will also need a limited amount of office equipment. When you visit an office equipment supplier you may be tempted by large leather armchairs and high quality desks but don't let any smart salesman talk you into buying items you do not really need. Potential customers are not going to be enticed by plush armchairs. They are only going to be interested in what you show them you can do on a screen and if you splash out a fortune on an expensive office it will simply be another drain on your resources. I am not suggesting that you should settle for an upturned crate and a couple of soap boxes but if you shop around you will find companies which can provide perfectly adequate furniture at a sensible price.

## BUYING A COMPUTER

There are a number of key items you will find you must have. The most useful office item you will acquire will be computer. Again you do not need to buy the most expensive model. You are going to want a machine which will enable you to manage your paperwork with a minimum of staff and in the shortest possible time. You should choose a computer which can run a wide range of programmes. You will initially need to buy a word processing programme and an accounts package. The word processor will be used for letter and scripts and it will enable you to build up a mailing list of your customer base. An accounts programme will save you the cost of employing anyone to do your day to day book keeping and it will give you all the facts and figures your Accountant will need to do an annual audit. Every business is obliged by law to keep written accounts recording every sale and purchase. If you employ other people you must also maintain a wages record and the government will send you lots of lovely forms which you will waste precious hours trying to complete. Paperwork is a curse in any creative business but if you choose the right computer programmes you can dramatically reduce the time required to do what must be done.

## MANAGING YOUR ACCOUNTS

When choosing computer programmes you should again avoid being persuaded to buy what the salesman wants to sell you. Decide what you need and don't buy anything which is too complicated. I made that mistake and bought an accounts programme which I had seen advertised as "very comprehensive". It was a good programme but I soon discovered that it was designed for use by Accountants who had different requirements to me and much more knowledge of accounting practice. It was far too complicated and did a lot of jobs which were no use to me. You want to be a film or video producer - not an accountant and you do not need a sophisticated accounts package which it may take you several weeks to understand.

You need a programme which is easy to operate and one which does not require any professional accounting knowledge. It should include a bought ledger, a sales ledger and an invoicing package. The bought ledger will enable you to list all the goods and services you buy. It will do all the donkey work for you and add up the totals and provide lists when they are required. If you give each of your productions a code number a good programme will also be able to analyse the entries bearing that code and tell you what each production you are working on has cost you to date. When tax returns and other joys have to be prepared it will print out the figures you need in minutes in stead of days. A sales ledger will enable you to do the same with everything you sell. I give all my productions code numbers so I can see at a glance how much money each production has brought in and what it has cost to make and supply. An accounts programme should also be able to produce statements so you can make sure people pay you on time. One of the most common reasons for business failures is bad cash flow resulting from a failure to get customers to pay bills on time. If you choose the right computer programmes you will find that you can send follow up statements and reminders of overdue accounts with a minimum of fuss and ensure your funds continue to flow.

## ISSUING INVOICES

The final item you will need in your accounts programme is an invoicing facility. You will not want to have to type out an individual invoice every time you need to send out an account. A computer will store a standard invoice form which you can design with your company heading and any layout you require. You can also pre-programme any items you sell on a regular basis so you do not have to enter them each time. For example, if you supply VHS video copies of a particular title or titles you can enter them into your computer memory and call them up in seconds in stead of having to re-enter every detail on each occasion. The computer will also add up your figures and that will also save you time. It will provide you with a list of the bills you have issued and the total amount due, and that is information you cannot afford to be without. So, buying a computer with basic accounting and word processing programmes is a good move but make sure it is easy to operate and supplied by a company which is not going to lose interest the moment the goods pass out of their doors.

## COSTING YOUR WORK

When you invoice your customers and when you work out quotes for work you are hoping to do, it is vital to ensure that your costings are correct. It is very easy to under-estimate costs and as a result find that at the end of the day you do not have enough cash in the bank to meet all your costs. It is a great mistake to under-price your services. Keeping costs in check is fine but cutting prices to the bone can be commercial suicide. Anyone can agree to make a video for next to nothing and many companies have gone into liquidation because the people running them have not had the ability to realistically assess their costs and price their services accordingly.

## WORKING OUT YOUR HOURLY RATE

Some costs are obvious. The items in your production budget, ranging from equipment hire to artistes fees, are not the sort of subjects you are likely to miss out when you prepare your quotations. You know what is involved in making a film or tape and will work out what each stage is going to cost you. What you may fail to include is an adequate allowance for your own time and for the depreciation of any equipment you have bought. It is a fatal mistake to under-estimate costs. When you have worked out what you are going to have to pay to make your programme check the figures and make sure you have not left out any key items. Have you included provision for your time? How much have you allowed ? What do you expect to earn over a year? Now, divide that by 12. You now know how much you expect to earn each month. Divide that again by 4 to find out the weekly total and by 5 to break it down into working days and finally by 8 to get your hourly rate. If you are going to stay in business you will need to recover at least that amount on everything you do or you will find you are working for nothing.

## OTHER COSTS TO CONSIDER

You should also allow for equipment depreciation. The items you buy will not last for ever. They will wear out and over 3 - 5 years and will need to be replaced and updated. You should work out how much that is going to cost over that period and include a proportion of the total figure as a depreciation charge on every job you do. You do not have to itemize it on your bill but you should allow for it in your costs.If you do not own any equipment you will no doubt be keen to buy it in due course. If you do not build a suitable sum into every production you will never own anything. Here are some other costs you will need to consider every time you price a job

*Accountants fees.* How much is your Accountant going to charge you to prepare your annual accounts and provide any other advice you may need ?

*Entertaining.* You will probably have to entertain potential customers and people whose business you have already won. The cost of doing that is another overhead charge which you will need to recover.

*Furniture, Fixtures and Fittings.* All these will wear out and your should budget for their replacement.

*Light and heat.* How much will you have to pay every year for your electricity gas and water ?

*Motor and travel.* Getting to potential customers and the travelling involved in everyday work will need to be considered in addition to journeys undertaken in the course of making individual productions.

*Postage.* Every time you write to someone looking for business or send out a completed video it will cost you money. It can all add up and, if you do not budget for it in advance,the overall cost may give you an unpleasant shock.

*Printing and Stationary.* You will need letter headings, invoices and envelopes and may also require brochures and other promotional material. The cost of designing and printing those items will have to be met.

*Telephone.* A figure for the rental of telephones, answering machines and all your call charges should be included in your overhead budget.

Before you submit a quotation to any potential customer, all these items should be borne in mind when you are calculating your figures. If you do not include them you may get the job because you have submitted a lower price than anyone else but at the end of the day you may go out of business because you have failed to consider all the costs involved in running your business.

Looking after the paperwork may sound a time consuming business and, if you do not plan your systems properly, it can be. If you work out what you want to do and get the right equipment to help you do it, you can minimise the time required and spend most of your hours making movies. Never under-estimate the importance of administrative work. You have a legal responsibility to keep records but what is even more important is that you will also find it impossible to run any successful business without them. A good system will help you to keep costs in check and to ensure you do not face any undue strain on your cash flow. It will enable you to plan your future investments by identifying areas where you are spending too much or those where more resources are required. You can achieve a great deal with a fairly small outlay.

## MAKING THE BEST USE OF YOUR TELEPHONE

You will also need a telephone answering machine or a link to a professional answering service. Answering machines are useful but you can lose business if customers know they are going to be answered by a machine every time they call. If you expect to be out a lot it may be worth considering subscribing to a telephone answering service. Originally pioneered for doctors, answering services now operate in most major cities. You can ask the telephone company to divert your calls to them. On a modern automatic exchange calls can be diverted automatically but in areas where the telephone exchange equipment is less up to date some engineering work may be required. The answering service will answer your calls with your name so the caller is unaware that it is not your office. You will then be given any messages when you ring in to find out who has called. It is not the ideal way to run a business. The ideal way is of course to be there yourself at all times time so you can deal with every query, but it is better than leaving a phone un-attended or relying on an answering machine day after day. One lost call can mean a considerable amount of lost business and, if a potential customer cannot speak to you, he may decide to call elsewhere.

## CHOOSING THE WORK YOU WANT TO DO

With your office base now established you can start the sort of work you intend to specialize in. You will by now have decided if you intend to sell your services as a freelance technician or to offer a complete production service working on film or video. Alternatively you may have decided to make your own programmes and offer them for sales to any interested parties. Let's consider each of those possibilities.

## MAKING MONEY FREELANCE

If you decide to make you money by working as a freelance technician when you have acquired the necessary technical skills,you will find that your success depends on establishing enough worthwhile contacts to keep you regularly employed. You will need to let people who employ freelance staff know that you are available. They in turn must be aware of the quality of your work and there again your showreel should help. Don't expect them to welcome you with open arms. There are thousands of good freelance technicians. Some get very little work but others manage to make a an extremely good living. You will find it is worth making contact by letter and by phone with film and television companies who use freelance staff. Try to arrange to show them what you have done make as many personal contacts as you can. It is much easier and nicer to deal with people you have actually met and if you get on well with them they are likely to remember you more than if you are just another name on a list. You will find you can get freelance work as a cameraman or as a camera assistant or as an editor or an assistant editor. Many sound recordists also work on a freelance basis. If you are not thoroughly experienced and confident that you can handle all the responsibilities of doing the top job you should offer you services as an assistant first and you will then avoid any possible embarrassment. It may also be worth asking you there are any vacancies as a holiday relief.

## OFFERING A PRODUCTION SERVICE

If you do not intend to work as a freelance technician you may decide to offer a full production service. You must then decide what customers you are going to try to attract.

There are several possibilities. You can target the tv companies. You can make videos and recover the production costs by selling and hiring copies,or you can undertake work which is sponsored by a commercial company. Let's look at each possibility in turn.

## MAKING PRODUCTIONS FOR TV COMPANIES

If you intend to make programmes and sell them to tv companies ( as opposed to working for them as a technician on their own programmes), you will need to tread very carefully. It may sound like an easy option. You have probably watched tv programmes and thought you could make programmes which are just as good and perhaps even better. In practice you will find it is quite difficult to sell anything to a tv company. They are principally interested in making money and it is often cheaper for them to stage a quiz show or a studio discussion on their own premises or to buy in an old movie than it would be for them to buy the sort of programmes you want to make. That is a general observation. Fortunately there are exceptions. Over the years I have sold a lot of programmes to tv companies and there is no reason why you should not do the same.

## WHAT TV COMPANIES WANT

You will often find it is easier to interest a tv network in a series of programmes than it is to sell them one. They are interested in slots - times on their schedules which they have to fill. If you can save them worrying about a half hour slot for eight weeks they may be more interested than if you can only fill a slot for one. If you study the programme schedules of your local networks you will find that a lot of the shows they transmit are presented in series. Even wild life films are often grouped together under a common series title and many documentaries are presented under one banner on a regular weekly or monthly basis. It is sometimes possible to sell material for use in one of those series. For example if you make a very good wild life video or a documentary on a subject no one else has done, you may be able to persuade a network or a satellite station to buy it and use it with their series title on the front and end. The alternative is to think of an idea for doing your own series and approach a tv company and try to pre-sell it.

## SELLING IDEAS TO TELEVISION

It is quite useless ringing up a tv network and saying you have a great idea for a new series. They will not want to know. It is equally useless writing to them with a basic idea unless it has been properly thought out and is well documented. First work out your ideas in your own mind. Think about them over a period. All new ideas seem great on the day they are first conceived but they do not always seem so good a few days later. So, if you have a good original idea for a tv series, think about and then put your ideas on paper. Has anyone done anything like it before ? If they have not, is there likely to be a reason for that? Perhaps it is a subject which is not of general interest or one which is going to be very expensive or difficult to film. If you still feel it could be a practical proposition, develop your ideas in detail. How many programmes could you produce? Six or eight is normally a minimum for a series and each will need to fill either a thirty or a one hour slot, including time for commercial breaks. Work out what you feel you would need to show in each programme and then how that programme would be structured so it has a beginning, a middle and an end. You can then do the hardest job of all and produce a detailed costing for the whole project.

In taking the steps we have just considered you will find out if your initial idea is as good it first sounded. If there are faults they may come to light as the work progresses. Doing all that work could take weeks or even months and when you have reached a stage which is advanced enough to know if you really do have a good idea or not, you may be able to try to arrange a preliminary meeting with the company you want to interest in your project. You can tell them that you have ideas for a series on whatever the subject is. You can enclose a synopsis explaining what each programme will be about and a summary of your estimated costs. If they express interest you may be commissioned to make a pilot programme. A pilot is a one off test to see if an idea works. If it meets with approval you could be in business but don't expect anything to happen overnight. Even if you have as superb idea and make a first class pilot programme, the stages I have outlined here could take anything up to three years to complete.

When you are considering ideas for making any films or videos it is important to remember that it is not just your interests that the programmes must satisfy. It is no use making programmes on subjects which appeal to you personally if they are unlikely to interest enough other people to prove commercially viable. TV companies in particular have to take a hard headed commercial approach. If they do not get mass viewing figures the sponsors who advertise with them will not buy air time. So any ideas you intend to present must be commercially acceptable to a fairly wide audience. In the United Kingdom the BBC and to a lesser extent Channel 4 offer an oasis of sanity in a sea of commercialism and regularly make and buy programmes on subjects which are only likely to interest fairly specialised minorities. Alas, they are exceptions to the general rule and even then you will be well advised to present any ideas you may have in the way I have described.

# MAKING FILMS AND VIDEOS FOR GENERAL SALE

Choosing subjects which will appeal to a large number of people is the secret of success in the second career possibility I mentioned above - making your own films and videos and recovering the cost of making them by selling and hiring copies. To make money you will need good distribution outlets. With general interest programmes you may be able to sell video copies to retail stores or you may try to get business by mail order. Again you will find the subjects you choose to film will have a considerable bearing on your commercial success.

## CHOOSING THE RIGHT SUBJECTS

If you decide you want to try making and selling your own films and videos to outlets other than television, you should first look at the titles which are already available. Your biggest potential market will be the sale of video cassettes. You will find they are sold at prices ranging from a few dollars in cut price retail outlets, to amounts which would meet the full cost of a week's holiday for two in a very lush hotel, for some specialist titles. You must decide if you want to try to get volume sales and go for popular subjects with mass appeal like sport or cookery. In either of those instances you may be able to recover part of your costs from video cassette sales and part from a sale to a tv network. Alternatively you could specialize in subjects which are not likely to appeal to a large audience but which could do well in specific market areas. Industrial training and medical subjects are two examples of areas where there is money to be made. Again you will need to study the markets. If you are dealing with a specialist subject you will probably also need to pay for specialist advice when you are preparing your scripts. You will not make a fortune overnight making any programmes speculatively and I would urge great caution before you take that course. Having issued that warning I can also tell you that over the years I have met many people who have made large numbers of programmes which were not paid for in advance and have managed to sell them extremely well.

## BUDGETING FOR PROMOTION

If you decide to make and sell your own programmes you will need to prepare two different budgets. First you must assess your production costs. You can do that in the way we have already explored. You will also need to prepare a promotional budget. The cost of promoting your completed programme may be as high or even higher than its initial production cost. You can make the best programme in the world but if no one knows it is available you will never sell it, so you must budget for getting all the publicity it requires. You can do that in several ways.

### ADVERTISING IN THE PRESS

Press advertising is one option. It tends to be expensive and you will need to choose the journals you use with great care. If you put an ad.in a national newspaper you may find you do not get a single reply but if you have a video on a specialist subject and advertise in the trade press you may do much better. For example, if you have videos on the history of music, educational journals may produce a worthwhile response. In your local library you will find books which list all the specialist trade journals in your country and overseas. You may find the cost of advertising one film or video is too high but if you have two or three to promote and are able to sell them at a reasonable price you may get a worthwhile number of replies. Do not expect thousands of enquiries and when the replies do come in don't assume everyone will buy. A one percent response rate to any advertisement is generally considered good by many of those in the industry who advertise regularly. If a journal has a 50,000 circulation you may only get a hundred replies but if you have a good product you can probably turn them to profit or establish a distribution network which will enable to you benefit and make a profit.

As I have said, press advertising is probably only worth considering if you have several programmes to offer. It is likely to prove most successful if you are selling a reasonably specialist product which can be targeted at a particular market and advertising repeatedly. General advertising in the daily press is only likely to prove worthwhile if you have a large number of titles and extensive distribution outlets. There are other ways of selling films and videos which you may find are more cost effective.

**SELLING BY DIRECT MAIL**

Direct mailing can also produce worthwhile results. Mailing companies will sell you lists of named individuals in various target areas. If you have a series of videos for school for example, they will sell you the names of Head Teachers and the addresses of so many thousand schools for an agreed fee. The addresses can usually be supplied printed on self adhesive labels or on a computer disc. If you intend to use the names more than once and thus get the maximum value for your investment, it is obviously best to choose the disk or photocopy the labels before they are sent out. Again, if you are making films or videos on specialist subjects, you may find direct mailing is a worthwhile exercise. When you send out a mail shot it is often worth following it up about a month later. You can telephone a cross section of the people you have mailed and should be able to discover if you are offering the right products or targeting the wrong people. Again much will be learned by experience but direct mailing is certainly another way of making money and one you may find it pays to consider.

## FREE PUBLICITY

If you want to get some free publicity you can submit copies of your videos for review by papers which include video reviews in their columns. Again you will often find some of the smaller specialist papers produce the best results. You may not even need to send a video to get a mention. Just supply a press release and, if possible,send some stills. A press release should explain what your programme is all about. Give a brief synopsis and a more detailed summary of the programme content and explain what it costs to buy and hire and where it can be obtained from. If you are asked to send a copy of the video to be reviewed the reviewer may also appreciate a copy of the script. It will make his or her job easier and should ensure that any quotations used are accurate. Don't expect every paper you approach to use the information you provide or to give you a review. Probably only a handful will do so but every little helps. You should not be upset if you get a bad review. There are very few destructive reviewers and they are often people who have never been able to achieve much themselves. Most reviewers take a pride in doing the job properly and will give the praise and possibly any criticism they feel is deserved in an objective way. Don't let that worry you. Any publicity is good publicity because it stimulates interest and that creates demand.

## FILM AND TV FESTIVALS

Another way of getting some publicity either free or for a fairly limited outlay is to enter your films or videos for one of the film or tv festivals which are organised all over the world every year. There are a lot of festivals and some are so badly organised they are not worth getting involved in.

Organisations like the American Film Institute and The British Film Institute may be able to provide you with details of forthcoming festivals and you will also find they are publicised well in advance in the film and video trade press. You will normally need to complete an entry form some months before the actual festival date so your title or titles can be included in the festival handbook. There is also likely to be an entry fee. It will probably not be excessive and you may find the publicity is worth paying for particularly if the festival is competitive and you manage to win something. Winning awards may not produce any great increase in revenue but the publicity will often manage to open up new markets and keep your name in front of people who ought to know you are around.

## PREVIEWING YOUR PRODUCTIONS

You will sometimes find potential customers will ask if they can preview a particular film or video before they buy it. If you are selling titles to the general public for a few dollars a time you may decide it is not worth offering them a free preview and simply agree to sell to them on a sale or return basis with payment on delivery or in advance. On the other hand if you are selling a specialist video at several hundred dollars a time it may be in your interest to let potential customers see what the video contains before they place an order. Experience suggests that you would be unwise to issue a new copy of the final version of your video for preview purposes. Most people are honest but there are some who will copy your tape and then tell you it is not what they require. You can combat dishonesty like that by producing special preview copies with the words *PREVIEW PURPOSES ONLY - NOT FOR GENERAL SHOWING* superimposed across the bottom of the screen throughout. That should stop anyone copying your programme and trying to sell it illegally. If they are really interested in what you have to sell, it will not put them off and they will ask to buy a copy without the preview title at the normal sale price.

So if you want to make videos on a speculative basis and recover your costs by selling and hiring copies,there are opportunities for you to make money. If you choose your subjects carefully and do some market research before you make your programmes you will do much better than if you simply rush off and make videos or films on the subjects which appeal to you personally. When you know there is a market for the kind of programmes you intend to make you can work out how you can best exploit it. That may involve press advertising or direct mailing leaflets with a reply coupon attached. You can back up your sales efforts by issuing press releases, arranging for your programmes to be reviewed and by entering film and video festivals. It will take you while to recover your investment but if you follow those basic rules and make superb quality programmes you could do well.

## ARRANGING A PRESS SHOW

You may decide that you wish to arrange a special preview showing of your film or video for the press and possibly for any major commercial concerns which might be interested. I decided to do that with my first film - the one about the work of artist John Hutton which I mentioned in an earlier chapter. I was starting my career and knew absolutely nothing about press shows and produced what I realize now was a very amateur press release. I did have the sense to choose one of the smarter preview cinemas for the showing and also to arrange a buffet with wines which I have since discovered is far the best way of encouraging the attendance of the press. The whole deal cost me rather more than I had spent making the film and at the time I felt I must be mad. It proved to be a good investment for a national newspaper did attend and much to my surprise devoted a column to the film under the headline "A young film maker to watch". I never discovered who that was ! That in turn lead to a telephone call from BBC2 asking if they could view a copy. They subsequently transmitted the film and I recovered all my costs and was able to arrange a number of overseas sales which produced a nice profit. So you may find a preview is worthwhile but it needs to be properly organised and invitations to the people you would like to attend should be sent out well in advance of the preview date.

## STAGING YOUR OWN PREVIEW

If you decide to organise a preview, you can either book a preview theatre where suitable film or video equipment is already installed, or you can book a hotel room and hire the film or video equipment yourself. The former course may prove easier and the results may look more impressive. If you do decide to do it all yourself make sure you have a run through several hours before your audience is due to arrive. I have heard of numerous occasions where hired equipment has failed to work at the last moment. If you are projecting a film make sure the room is adequately blacked out and have spare projection lamps to hand. Check to ensure there aren't any cables which late arrivals can fall over and place the loudspeaker above the heads of the audience alongside the screen and not on the floor so everyone can see and hear what you want to show them. If you are showing a video you may decide to use a video projector. If you are expecting an audience of less than 50 people I personally would suggest you should use three or four 27 inch tv monitors rather than a video projector. The colours will look better and for that number of people monitors will be perfectly adequate. Again set up everything well in advance.

## SELLING YOUR SERVICES TO SPONSORS

The last commercial possibility we are going to consider is selling your production services to sponsors who will meet all your production costs. We have already had some discussion on this subject earlier in this book but then you did not have the experience I hope you have got now. With your showreel and all the knowledge you have acquired making it you are now able to offer potential sponsors a rather better proposition.

The comments I made just now about only making films and videos on subjects which are commercially viable are particularly relevant when sponsors are involved. If a sponsor is meeting your production costs you will need to put your aims and objectives aside and use your skills to meet the wishes of your sponsor. That may be to promote a particular product or service, to show the attractions of a holiday resort or to train someone to do a particular job. I have undertaken sponsored commissions for many years and am no longer astonished by the range of subjects film and video producers are sometimes asked to film. I have found myself floating through the clouds in a hot air balloon, gasping for breath in a burning office and being seasick in ship which looked stable enough in port, all in the course of making sponsored films and videos. Again it's a very competitive field but it is also one which can offer excellent opportunities.

## WORKING WITH SPONSORS

Sponsors will normally expect you to provide a complete production service covering all stages from script to screen. You may find exceptions. There are always some sponsors who think they are born script writers. They will present you with their script where every other word will be " zoom" or "pan" and expect you to produce it. A lot of tact will be required. In fact the scripts for the most successful sponsored films and videos are usually the result of a team effort. The sponsor knows what he or she wants to say, show or promote. If that information is outlined in a brief you can then use your training and creative talents to turn it into a script. Before you start work you should agree a price for doing the job and sign a contract. That contract should state what the subject of the programme is and the type of format it is going to be produced on. An approximate duration should be given and the use to which the final film or video is going to be put should be outlined. If it is intended for non-theatrical use on video in the USA or the UK that should be mentioned. You will have to clear any music you use and contract any artistes who appear for a programme which is going to be used in a particular way and you will be well advised to ensure that your sponsor is aware of the uses for which his production will be cleared. If you make a promotional video for UK non theatric use and it suddenly appears on television you may find you face a massive bill from artistes or musicians. If you have not got the right words in the contract with your sponsor he or she may deny any knowledge of any restrictions and you will be left to pay out.

**WHO KEEPS CONTROL ?**

A sponsor will naturally wish to retain control of anything for which he or she has paid. In theory that could mean having a team of people from the commissioning firm breathing down your neck at every stage. In practice it is usually possible to agree to have one or two people involved throughout and to include provision for more detailed consultation at various stages of production. I always include provision for a sponsor to be able to ask for changes to be made to any script before filming starts. I then get their written agreement that all is in order before shooting begins. I also try to keep sponsors out of the cutting room until a fine cut is complete. I do that by arranging a fine cut viewing for anyone who wishes to attend and agreeing to make any alterations they may require as a result of that viewing. That does not mean they can change their mind on things they have already agreed to but it does give them freedom to change any shots they feel are not right and to make any other adjustments they may feel are required. In practice I rarely find they change anything at all. If they do ask for alterations it is sometimes an odd word of voice over commentary or some minor picture alteration. For example, not long ago we sat down with a sponsor to view a construction industry video which we had just completed. The sponsor was delighted with the programme but noticed that in one shot we showed a site worker who was not wearing a safety helmet. We were asked to replace that shot and were happy to do so. If you work closely with your sponsor at the initial planning stages, ask for one representative to attend when scenes are shot, and provide an opportunity for changes to be discussed before the final dubbing stage everyone should be happy with the end result.

## ARRANGING PROGRESS PAYMENTS

When you make programmes which are paid for by a sponsor you will not have to wait to recover your costs from the sale of copies. It is normal practice to seek progress payments as work goes ahead. You can ask for an initial payment - perhaps a third of the budget - to be paid on the signing of a contract. A further third can be invoiced when shooting starts and the balance on delivery of the first copy of the final edited version. You will sometimes find sponsors are unable to make progress payments because they do not have adequate funds in their quarterly budgets but on most occasions they will be quite happy to oblige.

So, by exploring the various markets open to you there is no reason why, with adequate knowledge and experience you should not be able to make money and build yourself an excellent career. How well you do depends on you. It is a tough world and you will not find it is any easier to win orders in film and television than it is in any other business but you will have the enormous benefit of doing work you enjoy. I wish you well and hope that this book has helped you to acquire enough basic knowledge to take your first steps. As those who have made a success of their careers in companies all around the world clearly demonstrate, if you persist with your ambition and have any talent, sooner or later you will meet with success.

# USEFUL CONTACTS:

## FILM SCHOOLS

*United Kingdom & Training Courses:*
**BKSTS (British Kinematograph Sound and Television Society)**, M6-14 Victoria House, Vernon Place, London WC1B 4DF
**Bournemouth & Poole College of Art**, Department of Photography, Film and Television, Wallisdown Road, Poole, Dorset BH12 5HH
**Bristol University**, Department of Drama, Film and Television Studies, Cantocks Close, Woodland Road, Bristol BS8 1UP
**Harrow College of the Polytechnic of Central London**, Northwick Park, Harrow HA1 3TP
**London International Film School**, 24 Shelton Street, London WC2H 9HP
**National Film and Television School**, Station Road, Beaconsfield, Bucks HP90 1LG
**Northern School of Film and Television**, Leeds Metropolitan University, 2-8 Merrion Way, Leeds LS2
**Ravensbourne College of Design and Communication**, School of Television, Walden Road, Chislehurst, Kent BR7 5SN
**Royal College of Art**, Department of Film and Television, Kensington Gore, London SW7 2EU
**University of Westminster**, School of Communication, 18-22 Riding House Street, London W1P 7PD
**West Surrey College of Art and Design**, Falkner Road, Farnham, Surrey GU9 7DS

*USA:*
The following publication is obtainable from Publications Dpt., American Film Institute, 2021 North Western Avenue, Los Angeles, California CA 90027:
**'American Film Institute Guide to College Courses in Film & Television'**

*Australia:*
**Australian Film, Television and Radio School**, P.O. Box 126, North Ryde, New South Wales 2113

# PRINCIPAL TELEVISION COMPANIES

*United Kingdom:*

**Anglia Television**, Anglia House, Norwich NR1 3JG

**Border Television**, Television Centre, Carlisle, Cumbria CA1 3NT

**British Broadcasting Corporation**, Television Centre, Wood Lane, London W12 7RJ

**British Sky Broadcasting Ltd.**, Centaurs Business Park, Isleworth TW7 5QD

**Carlton Television**, 101 St. Martin's Lane, London WC2N 4AZ

**Central Independent Television (East Midlands)**, TV Centre, Lenton Lane, Nottingham NG7 2NA

**Central Independent Television (West Midlands)**, Central House, Broad Street, Birmingham B1 2JP

**Channel Four**, 60 Charlotte Street, London W1P 2AX

**Channel Television (Guernsey)**, TV Centre, St. George's Place, St. Peter Port, Guernsey GY1 2BH

**Channel Television (Jersey)**, TV Centre, La Pouquelaye, St. Helier, Jersey JE2 3ZD

**GMTV**, The London Television Centre, London SE1 9LT

**Grampian Television**, Queens Cross, Aberdeen AB9 2XJ

**Granada Television**, Granada TV Centre, Quay Street, Manchester M60 9EA

**HTV Wales**, The Television Centre, Culverhouse Cross, Cardiff CF5 6XJ

**Independent Television News Ltd**, 200 Grays Inn Road, London WC1X 8XZ

**London Weekend Television**, South Bank Television Centre, Upperground, London SE1 9LT

**Meridian Broadcasting Ltd.**, 48 Leicester Square, London WC2H 7LY

**Scottish Television**, Cowcaddens, Glasgow G2 3PR
**Tyne Tees Television**, Television Centre, City Road, Newcastle-upon-Tyne NE1 2AL
**Ulster Television**, Havelock House, Ormeau Road, Belfast BT7 1EB
**Westcountry Television Ltd.**, Western Wood Way, Langage Science Park, Plymouth, Devon PL7 5BG

*USA:*

**ABC Television Division**, 1330 Avenue of the Americas, New York NY 10019
**CBS Inc.**, 51 West 52nd. Street, New York NY 10019
**National Broadcasting Company**, 30 Rockefeller Plaza, New York NY 10012
**The Fox Television Network**, 205 East 67th. Street, New York NY 10021
**Public Broadcasting Service**, 1320 Braddock Place, Alexandria, VA 22314-1698

*Australia:*

**ATN 7 Sydney**, TV Centre, Mobbs Lane, Epping, New South Wales 2121
**Australian Broadcasting Corporation**, G.P.O. Box 9994, Sydney, New South Wales 2001
**Australian Capital Television Pty. Ltd.**, Aspinall Street, Watson Act, Canberra 2602
**Network Ten Australia**, Northern Star Holdings Ltd., G.P.O. Box 10, Sydney, New South Wales 2007
**Nine Network Australia Ltd.**, 24 Artarmon Road, Willoughby, New South Wales 2068

There are also hundreds of other companies including satellite, cable and local stations. For a complete list check your local directories including those listed below.

## INDEPENDENT FILM & TV COMPANIES

There are thousands of independent producers of films and videos and they may well represent your best chance of finding your first job. For a complete list check your local library where useful reference books may include the following:

**'International Film & TV Directory'** published by EMAP Media Information, 33-39 Bowling Green Lane, London EC1R 0DA.
**'Kemps Film, TV & Video Year Book'** published by Reed Information Services, Windsor Court, East Grinstead House, East Grinstead, West Sussex RH19 1XA.
**'The International TV & Video Almanac'** published by Quigley Publishing Company, 159 West 53rd. Street, New York NY 10019.
**'The White Book'** published by Birdhurst Ltd., P.O. Box 55, Staines, Middlesex TW18 4UG.
**'Contacts'** published by The Spotlight, 7 Leicester Place, London WC2H 7BP.
**'World Radio-TV Handbook'** published by Glenn Heffernan, BPI Communications Inc., 1515 Broadway, New York NY 10036.